Confessing Conscience:
CHURCHED
WOMEN ON
ABORTION

Contributors

MARILOU AWIAKTA
SARAI SCHNUCKER BECK
COLLEEN C. CONANT
JUDITH CRAIG
ROBERTA KELLS DORR
JUDY MATHE FOLEY
JO KICKLIGHTER
LURLENE McDANIEL
SANDRA O. SMITHSON
MARTHA ELLEN STORTZ
JULI LOESCH WILEY

Confessing Conscience:
CHURCHED
WOMEN ON ABORTION

Phyllis Tickle
General Editor

ABINGDON PRESS
Nashville

Confessing Conscience: Churched Women on Abortion

Copyright © 1990 by Abingdon Press

This book is printed on acid-free paper.

Library of Congress Cataloging-in-Publication Data

Confessing conscience: churched women on abortion / Phyllis
Tickle, general editor; contributors, Marilou Awiakta . . . [et al.].
p.   cm
   ISBN 0-687-09388-0 (alk. paper)
   1. Abortion—Religious aspects—Christianity. I. Tickle, Phyllis,
II. Awiakta, Marilou, 1936-
HQ767.25.C66   1990
241′.6976—dc20   90-30080
                                                               CIP

The scripture quotation noted NIV is from the Holy Bible: New
International Version. Copyright © 1973, 1978, 1984 by The
International Bible Society. Used by permission of Zondervan Bible
Publishers.

MANUFACTURED IN THE UNITED STATES OF AMERICA

Contents

What We Would Like You to Know: A Preface...... 9

1 — Dear Children of My Daughter................. 13
Martha Ellen Stortz

2 — A Common Language............................27
Sarai Schnucker Beck

3 — Solidarity and Shalom............................39
Juli Loesch Wiley

4 — The Daughters of Heaven Are Weeping.....51
Colleen C. Conant

5 — And Rachel Wept....................................59
Lurlene McDaniel

6 — A Faith-Filled Talk of Life and Death.........69
Judy Mathe Foley

7 — A Bishop's Letter to Her Goddaughter.......77
Bishop Judith Craig

8 — Seed Corn Must Not Be Ground...............89
Marilou Awiakta

9 — Because I Have Been Loved....................103
Jo Kicklighter

10 — David and Bathsheba Have a Word
for Us...111

Roberta Kells Dorr

11 — In Him Was Life, John 1:4.................... 121

Sandra O. Smithson, O.S.F.

12 — Though We Walk Through the Valley of
the Shadow of Death: A Conclusion.......131

Phyllis Tickle

Confessing Conscience:
CHURCHED
WOMEN ON
ABORTION

What We Would Like You To Know:
Preface

A book is a door opened into the world of its creators' interior lives. Whatever any book is is what its authors and editors are, or are capable of presuming.

For its readers a book can be a sharing of humanness with impunity, a vicarious expanding of possibility with small risk; for its authors and editors it can sometimes be a Promethean agony of exchange between one's privacy and one's sense of community. For me, at least, this has been such a book.

The book you hold in your hand is a book which I, for one, would have never wanted to work on, left to my own devices; a book which, like the subject it treats, was never supposed to be. "All the world needs is another book on abortion," I had quipped on more than one occasion. Yet it exists, and you as its reader are entitled to know why, I think, before you commit yourself to pursuing it.

Each of the twelve of us who have committed ourselves to creating these essays has her own reason for joining the project. Each of us will, in the due course of things, reveal her own rationale. But as editor, the rules say, I must go first.

The old biblical phrase, "Blessed among women," has charmed and soothed me from my earliest memories. The melliferous words seemed, even in the dark corridors of childhood, to promise a future fullness of body, a golden time of crouching down to rise up again possessed of child.

I was born to make babies and knew it from the beginning. I make them easily, bear them lightly, and love them dearly. There are seven of them now, children of my body and fruit of our love, Sam's and mine, for almost four decades of mated life.

But there are the others as well, the children who haunt me and for whom, even in this time of my advancing age, I mourn and whose demise I have never accepted. They are the dead ones, the babies whom I miscarried, for I did miscarry. Over and over and over again I miscarried, until it seemed that for every child we brought to term, three had been lost.

Most of them were lost to me in a flood of waste and blood when they were half way toward safety. They were lost as children whose sex and shape I could plainly see as they floated away from me in the commode where I had to flush them or the old newspapers in which my hands had to wrap them, for in the 1960s and 70s they were children only to me. To the world beyond my cramping heart they were a medical accident of routine occurrence, part of the by-product of active living. The church said no words over them and perceived no loss from their nameless-ness; medicine reduced them to statistics in the record of my parity.

But I could never so reduce the memories of the swirling waters carrying my children away to sewage plants, nor could the shadows of their presence ever be exorcised from the dining tables of Christmases and

Thanksgivings, of birthdays and anniversaries. They still remain, like Banquo's ghost, as tangible and informative as any idea appertained, and as realized. It is they who persuade me that only women can bring to the issue of abortion not only the tools with which to conduct the debate, but the anguish out of which to sanctify it. And it is this latter task, finally, which has compelled me. Not another book about abortion. A book, rather, about living with the debate about abortion.

Each of us here has a story to tell—who among the sisterhood does not? Each has a position on the moral issue of abortion and usually on the political one as well, or else has consciously accepted the notion that she has no clear position and has to live with that torturous ambiguity. But that is not why any of us is here. The debate rages around us so furiously in the throats and placards of so many whose fury forgets the children as surely as it forgets our God that we have despaired of sacred resolution and would turn ourselves rather to the faithful of both sides whose pain wounds all humankind so ineffectually.

Each of us was asked, in the beginning, a quiet question. Each was asked: Once you have stated your position on legalized abortion, what is left to you as a Christian? "Christian, what now of your Christianity?" was the way one of us re-phrased it.

Some of us have assumed the epistolary form and have addressed ourselves to our descendants; some of us have moved in poetry; one of us, in the ancient legends of the native American.

We come to you from every walk of contemporary

femininity . . . journalists, theologues, housewives, professional activists, writers, religious.

We have arranged ourselves more or less by the number of our years in the belief that perspective broadens as experience is extended, and a book—certainly such a book as this—should grow broad near its conclusion, like a river arriving at its delta.

And, finally, one last thing. We span the spectrum of American denominationalism and care not a whit for those differences. All of us have bled and it is in the power and the ancient magic of that dark flow that we come, hoping to further the healing of a nation.

Phyllis Tickle
Advent 1989

1

Dear Children of My Daughter

Martha Ellen Stortz

Martha Ellen Stortz is associate professor of historical theology and ethics at Pacific Lutheran Theological Seminary, Berkeley, California. She holds a doctorate from the University of Chicago Divinity School. She has spoken and written widely on a variety of ethical issues, including bioethics, sexuality, human rights, feminism, and abortion.

Dear Children of My Daughter,

My thoughts keep turning back to the conversation we had at dinner during my last visit. Your mother and I were trying to explain to you the intensity of the abortion controversy during the last decades of the twentieth century, and you simply didn't understand.

I have to smile, because your utter incomprehension delights me—and reminds me that what I wished for my grandchildren was that the whole controversy be foreign to you. When I entered adulthood, as you are now, the controversy divided husbands and wives, families, communities, and churches. You cannot imagine the anger and rage vented on the subject! And, as your mother and I discovered in our comical but futile efforts to make the past somehow present, you really cannot understand. Advances in reproductive technology, shifts in mores, changes in the church itself have rendered the debate moot. Your incomprehension elates me—this is what we wanted for our children and grandchildren. But, at the same time, your incomprehension saddens me, because the abortion controversy was so much a part of our formation, painful but powerful. It was not so much an issue which your mother and I had to confront, but an occasion for examining critically our faith in God and in the people whom God had called together to be "church." The whole abortion controversy challenged us to speak, live out, and recognize the limits of that faith. What your mother and I realized, as we talked later alone and into the gray hours before dawn, was that if our children and grandchildren would be a part of that community of faith, then you must understand how we tried to embody that faith in this most wrenching controversy. More than understand, you must judge, forgive, and gain from our efforts to be the faithful people we are called to be. Our silence on the subject only diminishes you.

Your mother and I spent hours that night grilling each other. How had we kept all of this from you: by consensus or coincidence? More difficult, *why* had we kept this from you: for your protection or for ours? It is important that you read that chapter of our lives; this letter is its first draft. It is an attempt to explain, probably as much to myself and to your mother as to you, the whole controversy around abortion. But more than explanation, this letter is an attempt to confess, again as much to ourselves as to you, what we believed, then and now, about God and God's people, and how that belief formed and informed that portion of our lives and that piece of your histories.

In the political world, the abortion controversy was cast in terms of rights. Competing universes of rights polarized debate: the rights of the fetus and the rights of the woman. There were two sides, and one lined up facing the other antagonistically; those defending the rights of the fetus and those defending the rights of the woman. It was a courtroom drama: *Fetus v. Female,* with "We the people" playing plaintiff and defendant, judge and jury simultaneously.

Language did nothing to clarify the debate; indeed, language only fueled the fires of rage. Those defending the rights of the fetus termed their position "pro-life," implying that all opponents were "anti-life." Those defending the rights of the woman termed their position "pro-choice," implying that all opponents were "anti-choice." Everyone, regardless of position, fell under subjugation to the tyranny of language.

Two Supreme Court decisions set the stage for outright war. In its 1973 decision in *Roe v. Wade*, the Court ruled that the constitutional "right to privacy . . . is broad enough to encompass a woman's decision whether or not to terminate her pregnancy." The right was deemed to be fundamental, and the state could intervene to protect the life of the mother and to protect the life of a fetus in the last stages of a pregnancy. A trimester framework described fetal development and determined at what points a woman's right to privacy prevailed and at what points the state could intervene.

Roe met with both support and censure. Supporters hailed it as a giant step on the road to reproductive freedom for women. Challengers charged the decision with legalizing murder and sought legislative and juridical redress. Redress came from the Supreme Court itself in a 1989 decision in *Webster v. Reproductive Health Services*. The Court supported a Missouri statute which proposed a variety of measures allowing states to regulate abortions. The controversy moved into fifty state legislatures.

The *Webster* decision made it impossible for legislators *not* to take a stand on the issue of abortion and face the electoral consequences. But legislators were not the only ones under scrutiny. Church leaders too found themselves seated squarely in the midst of the controversy. Constituencies questioned anxiously and urgently: What does the church have to say about abortion? Frustrated and faithful church leaders hurried into studies on the subject. The problem was acute.

It was at this point that I entered the fray: a woman, a layperson, a seminary professor, a teacher of ethics and history at a small Lutheran seminary in Berkeley, California. How would I respond? In answering, I was not seeking to make a personal stance alone; I felt myself inalterably part of the community. The question presented itself: How might we as the community called church respond? And before I could even address that question, I had to consider a prior question: What did it mean to be a community called church?

As I considered this question, I turned to the event constitutive of that community: baptism. I'd participated in dozens of baptisms, including a first one, beyond memory, but recorded carefully and observed annually. What struck me about those countless ceremonies was the name bestowed: it was not "Martha Ellen Stortz, daughter of Margaret and Cliff Stortz," or even "Martha Ellen Stortz, member of Zion Evangelical Lutheran Church," but "Martha Ellen, child of God." What struck me was the concreteness of the sacrament itself: water and washing. What struck me was the significance of the sacrament as a rite of initiation: physical and spiritual integration into a Christian community. A new understanding of the sacrament opened up to me. Far from being a private ceremony, whose chief significance was in the spiritual realm of faith, baptism assumed new importance as a public ceremony concerned with both physical and spiritual dimensions of Christian life. It was a public exchange of promises: these promises bound believer and community in both body and soul. Baptism made our lives—in body and spirit—a matter of communal concern.

The early church was clear about the physical aspects of that communal concern. Childrearing was not a nuclear family affair, nor death a private sorrow, nor poverty an individual struggle. Almsgiving, ministry to the sick and dying, care of widows and orphans were evidence of the church's support for the physical welfare of its members. This was part of what it meant to be a community called church.

With this new insight into an ancient sacrament, I turned to the abortion controversy: How might we as a community called church respond? Immediately, I realized that the terms set by debate in the political realm were inadequate to express the depth of what it meant to be this kind of community. We could not make a stand "pro-life" or "anti-life," "pro-choice" or "anti-choice," "pro-life" or "pro-choice," because those were not the only places to stand. As Christians, we had a distinctive understanding of baptized community that made it impossible for us to use those terms with quite the connotations they had in the political debate. Beneath the political debate were assumptions that we as Christians had to challenge: (1) an implicit individualism; (2) an isolation of abortion from surrounding domestic and economic contexts; and (3) finally, an understanding of "life" unreflective of our deepest convictions. You will pardon an old woman's pedantry as I elaborate each point in turn.

First, there was an individualism implicit in the controversy which, once I had identified, I simply had to reject. From the pro-choice camp came a defiant possessive individualism: "Our Bodies, Our Selves." As a historian, I understood all too well the experience behind such a spirit: those distant centuries in which women were regarded as chattel and those not-so-distant centuries in which women were the psychological, emotional, and economic property of their fathers and husbands. It was a history that filled me with rage and sorrow. But the possessive individualism that pro-choice people proposed as an alternative ran counter to the spirit of the community we were called to be.

From the pro-life camp came an even more frightening form of individualism. There, concern for the life of a child ended with its birth. There was no concern for the community into which a child might be born; there was no attempt to *be* the community into which a child might be born. The "right to life" in practice seemed to begin at conception and end at birth. Again, an atomistic individualism pervaded the pro-life position as well, counter to the spirit of the community we were called to be.

I was fighting an individualism engrained in our culture, buttressed by a tradition in political philosophy that regarded people as free only as they were free from the communities and relationships that had formed them. Each person existed as a universe unto herself, surrounded by her rights. The chief and only threat to her was another person with another and competing universe of rights. Relationships between such potentially antagonistic individuals were by definition difficult; relationships were contractual and subject to terminal negotiation. It was a lonely and alienating portrait of human nature and of human community.

As I began to think about the community called church, I realized that our understanding of freedom came, not from being free of all communities and all relationships, but precisely from being in a new relationship with God and in that community of people bound and sealed by baptism. Relationships were not between potential competitors, but between children of God; they were not contractual, but covenantal. Ours was a vastly different portrait of human nature and of human community.

And yet, as I began to look at the community called church, I saw that an ethos of individualism had eroded the fabric of community within congregational life. Families existed as independent and autonomous units, and those not within a family unit—singles, divorced people, single parents, elderly widows and widowers, gay and lesbian folk—were ostracized. Minding one's own business had become an ecclesial ethic. Advocacy, bearing one another's burdens, sharing goods in common had evaporated. I had to confess that the church looked far more like a loose federation of religious virtuosí than a community of baptized believers. We were caught in the gap between who we were and who we were called to be.

Second, the controversy tended to treat abortion in isolation from its surrounding domestic and economic contexts. Pro-choice activists focused narrowly on the choice *not* to have children, which was a choice to secure abortion. Lost was any broader consideration of securing whatever would make it possible for women to be able to choose to have their children: welfare, health care, and education. Pro-life activists focused on the life of a child from conception to birth. Lost was any broader consideration of the right to life of children already born.

As I began to think about the community called church, I felt compelled to raise these broader considerations. Because we professed a physical, as well as spiritual, concern for the members of our community, we had to raise issues of sex, marriage, and family; issues of gender, race, and class. We had to point out that proposed regulation of abortion would not alter the availability of the services to wealthy women, who could afford travel to a state with liberal laws. Such regulation affected only poor and rural women, who could ill afford travel and cost of services. We had to emphasize that the costs of childbearing and childrearing fell increasingly upon the nuclear family and often upon the mother alone. We had to reiterate that the primary responsibility for contraception still fell on women; we had to remind that there were still not safe and reliable means of contraception. We had to protest federal cuts in welfare, health care, and education. Ours was a vastly different understanding of the context surrounding abortion.

And yet, as I looked at the community called church, I saw a community with confused ideas about sex, marriage, and family. I saw a community in terminal denial about sexuality, unwilling to discuss honestly sexual desire, sexual behavior that led to conception, available contraception; unable to speak some hard words about abstinence. One of my students at the time put it well: "We tell our kids sex is awful—but you'd better save it for the person you marry!" I saw misogyny in the churches: women barred from ordination, women ordained but without call. I saw a disregard for children in the segregation of age groups within parish life, the fear of children "disrupting" our solemn assemblies, the practice of an "inclusive" language that excluded the youngest members of our communion. I had to confess that the church participated in many of the prejudices that plagued the world. We were caught in the gap between who we were and who we were called to be.

Finally, the use of the word "life" itself troubled me deeply. The term was thrown about with a good deal of imprecision—scientific, moral, theological, or otherwise. "Life" itself was deemed an incontestable and absolute good. Pro-choice activists tried to argue for the primacy of the "life" of the woman; pro-life activists tried to argue for primacy of the "life" of the fetus. I was left in the dust, still puzzling over what kind of baggage might be packed behind the term "life" itself.

As I began to think about the community called church, I realized that all life is given as a gift by God, both the life of a woman and the life of a child. I firmly believed that God's intention for the life God both created and gave was life in community, life in well-being, life in relationship, life lived out in faith, hope, and love. This kind of life did not begin automatically with conception—indeed, I could see painful evidence that thousands of children have lived and died without ever having received this gift of life at all. This kind of life was not something we could defend at conception and desert at birth. Rather, we were called to create the physical and spiritual possibilities for the nurture and sustenance of this kind of life. Baptism demanded nothing less than this kind of stewardship.

And yet, as I looked at the community called church, I could see that our stewardship was lacking. We were caught in the gap between what we were and what we were called to be.

The question burned in my head: How might we as the community called church respond in the abortion controversy? The response I wanted the church to make was this: "We as a church censure the practice of abortion; therefore, we agree to adopt all unwanted children and to work for a world in which all children will be wanted and all parents will have the physical and spiritual means to want them." I saw how far the church was from being able to make the response it should have made. Therefore, I pressed the church to make the only response it could: a response of profound repentance. We were not the kind of community we were called to be, and abortion existed in that gap, a judgment upon all of us.

Your mother and I were caught in between positions we wanted to take, given what the church was called to be, and positions we had to take, given what the church in fact was. We found it impossible to endorse abortion as a positive good, and yet we found it imperative to ensure that women of all races and classes, in any situation, had free access to medically safe abortion procedures. We found ourselves repenting the state of our churches, our narrow prejudices and our grudging stewardship of life, and yet we were desperately committed to the task of moving them from where they were to where they were called to be.

Were these appropriate and faithful responses? That is the question that has troubled us ever since. To choose a position that was merely "pro-life" or "pro-choice," in the terms set by the controversy, would have been easier. In choosing a pro-community position, as your mother and I did, we had to confront both our calling and our short-falling. We had to embrace each with realism and with hope.

I give to you both the calling and the short-falling, gift and challenge. I give to you the question, still burning: Were these appropriate and faithful responses? Judge us with compassion—for judge you must. This chapter in our lives is now yours.

My love, dears
Your Grandmother

2

A Common Language

Sarai Schnucker Beck

Sarai Schnucker Beck, who holds a Master of Divinity degree from Yale Divinity School, was born in Lancaster, Wisconsin, and is on the Task Force on Abortion of the Presbyterian Church (USA), charged with writing a new abortion position for the church. Her thinking on this subject of abortion has been influenced by her experience as a working mother and by a class she has taught since 1980 on women in the history of the Christian church. The Reverend Ms. Beck is currently Parish Associate at Germantown Presbyterian Church in Germantown, Tennessee.

This book is about the influence of the abortion controversy on the lives and practice of believing Christian women in 1990. As an "approach" to the subject, each of us has been asked to "imagine that you are writing for your grandchildren or for young persons who will come of age in thirty years." This approach I find that I cannot make, for as much as my children may want to know in thirty years why I have chosen to become involved in this issue, or as much as I might then want to explain my choices, right now my most urgent need is not to communicate with my children or imagined grandchildren, but rather to understand and talk with women on the "other side," friends with whom I disagree. I want to understand why we seem to talk past each other, why our feelings are so strong, why our patience is so thin. And once we've understood, then perhaps together we can find a way to bridge this chasm that we allow to exist between us.

So, first I want to tell you, not my children, the story of who I am and where I think my views on abortion might have come from. I start with this personal narrative because I believe that individual stories are important, both to an understanding of why women choose or refuse abortions, and to an understanding of the position each of us takes on this issue. I am convinced that the insights we need in order to reach out to each other will come from the details of our own stories. After this narrative section, I want briefly to state my position on abortion, and then to go on to a letter I wrote recently, not to an imagined future, but to a present friend with whom I disagree.

My Story

I am thirty-three years old, a fourth-generation Presbyterian minister, married to Frank, a second-generation Presbyterian minister. We have two small boys, Christjahn and Daniel, who in the fall of 1989 are five and three and a half. Like most women, I came to marriage and family with a background of particular experiences, beliefs and needs, all of which collided with the reality of children. It is probably somewhere in the collision that I can begin to locate my views on abortion.

First, I was born shy. I used to think that I became shy as a result of social awkwardness and the possession of a little more intelligence than it was considered appropriate for a girl to have growing up in a small town in Missouri. But now that I have children of my own, I can see that some of us are born shy, born to be watchers before we are doers, born to get our energy from being alone. This need to be alone has become more pronounced in the last five years, as it has been less and less met.

I was also born into a political culture that places a high value on the individual and on individual rights, and into a particular family in which individuality, even uniqueness, was honored and preferred. I remember having no doubt that we were "different" when I was a child. My father was a professor, my mother taught, we were "liberal" Democrats in a time and place when this was not always popular. All three of my brothers and I played stringed instruments, for heaven's sake. We were different. And yet personal autonomy was sometimes hard to find, particularly for a female first child. I suspect that my father was more comfortable when we were different in *his* way and not in our own; I was often easy prey to his inducements to change my mind. So I grew up valuing nonconformity and making up my own mind about all kinds of issues, and yet often having to fight for the right to do so. To this day, my favorite refrain is, "Nobody tells me what to do!" Nothing brings on my anger more quickly than being given an order, and nothing makes me stand up more quickly than being told to sit down.

All of these elements—my comfort with nonconformity, my need for autonomy and solitude, our individualist culture—have had to coexist with my need for consensus and the value I have learned of community, for I am learning over the years the art of being a good steward of family and friends. I sometimes experience the value of relationships and community as being in conflict with my own needs; but I am schooling myself to see, not conflict, but rather one more instance of one of the basic tensions that exist within all Christians—the tension of the individual who knows that she stands alone before God and yet who knows at the same time that she exists only within the whole community that is the Body of Christ.

In any case, all these bits and pieces came into sharper focus when my children were born, and I began the ongoing struggle to balance children and work. Such a balance has been difficult for me to achieve, feeling as I do that I was "born" to work, and feeling at times that I don't even exist when there is no time to read and reflect and learn. Yet I know also that no one can love children as well as a parent, and that my boys and I both need this time together. By now, their presence has become so much a part of me that I can't work without them in the house. (This pattern will have to be relearned when they go to school.) But I also hear a cry from my own heart when I read Adrienne Rich's words about Marie Curie, "Her wounds came from the same source as her power."[1]

Position on Abortion

Of all that I write here, I find this the hardest to commit to paper. In part, I know that once I've stated my views, others will find them a reason to resist, rather than an invitation to share. In part, I have found my position on abortion to be unexpectedly fluid, responding to arguments from both sides. The discovery has been very surprising, for I had thought I knew what I thought. Briefly, however, I support the ability of women to make their own decisions about abortion. I do so because: (1) there are occasions, perhaps many occasions, when abortion is the lesser of evils. On those occasions, the pregnant woman will bear a great burden, perhaps the greatest burden, whatever decision is made; (2) restrictive laws cannot adequately take into account the complexity of the dilemma confronting each pregnant woman; (3) I fear the consequences of a

---

1. "Power," in *The Dream of a Common Language: Poems 1974–77* (New York: Norton, 1978).

restrictive law both for women forced to find a means to abortion beyond that law, and for a society with a law which so many will find it necessary to break; and (4) I trust most women to make responsible decisions. These obviously do not exhaust the reasons for which one might support an essentially "pro-choice" position, but from my own experience and work they are the ones I find most compelling.

On the question of the role of law, by the way, I have found Mary Ann Glendon's *Abortion and Divorce in Western Law* to be very helpful in my own pursuit of a common language with which women who disagree might carry on conversation about abortion. In this country, we have become accustomed to thinking there is no legislative middle ground. Consequently, we often avoid the effort to reach any theological or ethical middle ground for fear that we will lose the legislative battle. Using a comparative legal approach and drawing on examples of abortion legislation from European countries, Glendon suggests that it *is* possible to write a sort of "compromise" legislation which at the same time both "tells a story" of the value of human life and the importance of community, and yet also allows for the opinions and behavior of those who "do not share or cannot live up to this ideal."[2]

Letter to a Friend

Dear _____,

We share so much, and yet we are so much at odds. I avoid even talking about abortion with you because I

---

2. *Abortion and Divorce in Western Law: American Failures, European Challenges* (Cambridge, Mass.: Harvard University Press, 1987), p. 141.

know that we will inevitably clash, and the friend I value and respect will become a stranger, in the same instant in which I, too, disappear for you.

And yet we do share, not just trivial incidentals but important, perhaps central, feelings and beliefs. It's even been a sort of trend recently among writers about abortion to emphasize points of agreement. I read an article recently by Daniel and Sidney Callahan, for example, a "pro-choice" advocate and a "pro-life" advocate who are married to each other. Based on their studies, they list four areas of common ground: (1) both sides are trying to form a different kind of synthesis, using both "liberal" and "conservative" ingredients; (2) both sides increasingly distrust a kind of "libertarianism" that would completely separate the individual from the community; (3) both sides are uncomfortable with their labels—"pro-life" and "pro-choice"; and (4) both sides are concerned about the circumstances that lead or drive women to abortion.[3]

It's nice to know that we're part of a trend, and I agree with the Callahans' perceptions, but you and I also share some other perceptions. Perhaps if we pay closer attention to our common ground, we can find a new way to speak, a new language that will bring us together, a new place to stand.

I wonder, sometimes, why this is so important to me. Perhaps it is because I'm a woman, and women seem more inclined to put energy into maintaining a complex

---

3. "Breaking Through the Stereotypes," *Commonweal*, October 5, 1984, pp. 522-23.

web of relationships. Perhaps it is because I'm a Christian and struggle against our American tendency to fragment the Body of Christ. I am convinced that God intends in some way that we disagree, because it has always been in disagreement that the Church has refined its understanding of God and God's relationship to creation. But I do not believe that God intends the levels of distrust and hostility to which this abortion discussion has fallen. We must seek a path to discussion, not destruction. Perhaps that path is through a recognition of what we share.

First, we share faith in God and faith in Jesus Christ as Emmanuel, God-with-us in human form. Not everyone involved in the abortion discussion shares this faith, but you and I do, and I have to believe that here we agree more than we disagree. There may be differences in *how* we interpret Scripture, but surely these are differences more of form than of content.

Because of our faith, I think that we also share a belief that all of life is important—human beings, animals, plants, germs in the sea, birds in the air, all are part of God's creation. For me, this has come to mean, more now than in the past, taking with great seriousness the potential human life that is the fetus. But for both of us, I believe that it also means taking with great seriousness the present life of a woman in a difficult and complicated situation. We talk about these two "lives" making "conflicting" claims, or "competing" claims, as if they were adversaries, with one soon to be a winner and the other a loser. Perhaps it would be better to think of the fetus and the mother as having "concurrent" claims. That is, both claims occur at the same time and both are important. They are perhaps not always claims of equal weight—at times the potential life that is the fetus may have a stronger claim, and at times the mother's claim may override. We may disagree about how to adjudicate these claims, but I am convinced that you and I agree that life is valuable because it is given by God.

I am convinced also that you and I share some feelings that are born of our sinfulness rather than our faith. For instance, I think we both tend to think of the other side as the "enemy," alien, wholly other, someone totally incomprehensible and essentially wrong. Incredibly, when we women see the "enemy" in other women, this repeats in a different form the very sin of sexism of which we have all been victims for so long. That is, we see the one who is different as one who is also less than, lower than, unable to. We have to stop separating ourselves from and abstracting the "other," even though not all of us on either side will be able to, or even want to do so. It is here, perhaps, as much as anywhere, that faith enters my own internal dialogue. I believe, although at times inadequately, that I will meet God in this "other," partly because I have met God in you. And surely if we are all children of God and bearers of God's image, then the differences in experiences and views between us should be valued, not shunned or suppressed.

I think we also share, in our sinfulness, in a large element of fear. Sometimes I am afraid, for instance, that you might say something that will disrupt my beliefs or change my life. We both know that words are powerful, and that they can create belief as much as reflect it. What if you say something that re-creates me? I am afraid that I will find out I've been wrong. I am afraid that I'll lose something important—a husband, perhaps, or my ability to choose my own life, to write my own story. I am afraid that the choices I've made will turn out to have been the wrong ones. Because I am afraid, I keep my distance from you. I believe that you are afraid, too.

But I also believe that to some degree we can overcome our sinfulness, because of our love for and care of each other and of the world's children, a love that is grounded in God's love for us. And so I think that finally we share the dream of a common language. I first heard of this dream in a poem by Adrienne Rich, "Origins and History of Consciousness," in which she describes the writing of poetry. The "true nature of poetry," she says, is "[t]he drive to connect. The dream of a common language."

It is this last that I think we share. The drive to connect. The dream of a common language. I admit that I experience my own struggle to connect with you as equal parts "drive" and reluctance. This whole letter is not easy for me to write because every time I reach out in my mind to grasp your hand and make a connection, my mouth keeps wanting to say to you, "You're wrong! You're just wrong!" But nonetheless I feel from both of us, from many of us on both "sides" of this issue, a drive to connect, a need to stop being enemies and to start working together, a dream of a common language. My prayer is that as we begin to talk and to really listen to each other, to hear our own stories and the stories of the women who face difficult decisions in their lives, we will learn, and perhaps even begin to teach, a common language. And then we can start to write a new story of what it means to be women of God. Let me hear.

All love,
Sarai

3

Solidarity and Shalom

Juli Loesch Wiley

Juli Loesch Wiley has been active in a variety of social justice causes: peace education, prison ministry, women's shelter, United Farm Workers boycotts. She is a contributing editor at *New Oxford Review* and a frequent columnist for *National Catholic Register/Twin Circle*. Her articles appear in *Commonweal, Social Justice, Catholic Worker, Thirty Days,* and *Fidelity*. She is a member of Feminists for Life, on the advisory board of the Pax Christi Center on Conscience and War, a founding member of Seamless Garment Network, a board member of JustLife Political Action Committee, and press coordinator for Rachel's Rescue. She has been arrested eleven times for nonviolent direct action.

I was twenty-one years old in 1972. By that time, a year before *Roe v. Wade*, I was aware that practically all of my female friends—at least those whom I knew well enough to know such an intimate detail about—had already aborted a first baby. Some, a second.

I had not. But this was not because my sexual life-style was any different or better than theirs: the late sixties and early seventies were the heyday of life-style experimentation and the sexual revolution, and I was out there skirmishing like much of the rest of my generation. It's just that I never became pregnant.

I also knew that we were all good women, caring and sensitive, in fact quite biophilic, pacifists or near-pacifists mostly. ("Make Love, Not War.") We did not act out of malice. And such good women do not commit murder. Therefore abortion could not be murder.

The Church of my childhood, the Catholic Church, I had left behind several years before. It seemed to me that the Church had rules for sexuality that bound like iron bands, and rules for war and the military that were more like *rubber* bands. This apparent inconsistency robbed Church "Sanctity of Life" arguments of moral legitimacy in my eyes. I also sided with the secular feminist movement against my Church on virtually every disputed question.

So I got out.

Like many abortion rights advocates, I saw an unwanted pregnancy as an adversary situation. On the one hand, you have a woman in crisis, a woman big as yourself and just as articulate. On the other hand, you have an embryo or fetus the size of a cashew, a walnut, or a pear. The one, you know. The other, you don't. Choosing sides, you choose the woman. End of argument.

By the mid-1970s I had been involved with most of the movements on the "progressive" agenda: United Farm Workers, anti-Vietnam war, anti-nuclear, environmentalism, and feminism—including feminist spirituality of the Goddess-reverencing sort.

In my meditations the notion of a Godhead "in whom we live and move and have our being"—a phrase Paul used to describe our relationship to Christ—suggested a distinctly maternal picture. *Pater Noster*, the Holy Roman Empire God who looked to me like Blake's *Urizen*, all beard and biceps, had no womb for us. So the God in whom one could "live and move" like a baby in its watery womb world, must certainly be a Goddess.

But I also had a vague notion that if this Goddess were, God forbid, a feminist, and I were the fetus, she might reject, destroy, abort me—and I wanted so much to be born! That sent a chill through me. I set aside the Goddess meditations and went back to being a Christian-of-a-sort, a Christian as far as feminism would let me, a Christian without definition.

I set aside thinking much about abortion, too, for years on end, perhaps because I did have this disquieting tendency in unguarded, intuitive moments to see myself as the *embryo*: on the wrong side of solidarity, on the wrong end of the gleaming technology, and, surely, on the wrong side of the argument.

Progressive religious peace-and-justice centers turned out to be ideal places to hide out from the abortion issue in the 1970s. Catholic, Christian, interfaith, whatever: I knew of "nonviolence" communities which avoided having a serious discussion of abortion-as-violence for a solid silent decade. We did not search our sacred gospel or our almost-sacred Gandhi for deep perspective, nor did we inventory our own resources for ways to offer a life-giving or a life-defending response.

Surrounded by pictures of My Lai and Hiroshima children, we would not look steadily (who could?) at who or what was at the business end of a suction curette.

At some point in the late seventies, though, I experienced a turn-around. It would be a long story to explain all the factors in my conversion, for they were not clear and all-at-once, but subtle and cumulative. But once a turn-around had been made, once I began to go public with it in the Christian Left, everything changed. To put it briefly, all hell broke loose.

First, I must explain the basic shift in perception which caused me to reject my former toleration of abortion.

I saw, first of all, that the whole "sexual revolution" failed to live up to its claims. I began to see casualties: women ripped off by fly-by-night relationships; men and women uneasily aware that they'd used somebody, or that they'd *been* used; people becoming cynical, or downright callous (though we'd been told that greater sexual "openness" would help us to be more *in touch,* more *compassionate).*

Above all, I saw women hurt, and hurt badly, by abortion. Women friends who'd expressed only "relief" after obtaining abortions five or six years before, were telling me that they were now barely able to cope

43

with the undercurrents of emptiness and pain in their lives. Numbness—a chosen numbness—had replaced sensitivity; avoidance—also chosen—replaced awareness; euphemistic, evasive locutions replaced the one-syllable frank language upon which we had formerly prided ourselves.

I saw romantic relationships which were supposed to be saved by abortion, split; I saw careers which were supposed to be enabled by abortion, fail to materialize or fail to satisfy. I saw appalling heart-hurt.

All of our holistic philosophies had a hole, and the hole kept getting bigger, not smaller.

Yes, I'd once made the assumption that an unwanted pregnancy was an adversary situation between a morally significant woman and a not-as-significant embryo; and of course the stronger currents of solidarity in me said, "side with the woman."

I now saw that pregnancy is not an adversary relationship; it's a mutual relationship. The woman and the unborn life she carries are not rivals; they in fact share the consequences of good treatment or bad. Their well-being does not naturally compete: it naturally coincides. It was not "woman versus fetus": it was wholeness *for both* or injury *for both*.

The solidarity of woman and embryonic child, the "sharing" of the consequences of good treatment or bad—it made sense in terms of everything else I believed in: the discipline of nonviolent conflict resolution; the insights of ecology ("Everything is connected"); women's health and wholeness advocacy. I felt as if I had become a "pro-lifer" not despite, but because of my commitment to values on the "progressive" side of the political/social spectrum. I had become, in plain words, *consistent.*

At the same time, here I was, a feminist with a skeptical view of "sexual and reproductive rights." A Left-Liberal who sided—on one subject, at least—with Jesse Helms. I had become, in plain words, a freak.

I felt a strong thirst for dialogue with people on the Left. But the white secular Left was, simply, *not interested.* "Abortion rights" had become so nearly an absolute that discussion itself was taken for treason. Requesting a two-sided dialogue was seen as an offensive and provocative act in itself.

I'd started a little group in 1979 called *Prolifers for Survival* ("P.S.") for the explicit purpose of waging protracted dialogue about abortion within the peace community, and, conversely, for pushing a moral critique of war and the nuclear arms race within the pro-life community.

Why was I unprepared when civil libertarians from the National Lawyers' Guild threatened to have P.S. people arrested on the public street for *leafletting?* Why was it stunning to me when peace-and-justice folks cut off our microphone at a public meeting and chanted to drown us out when we attempted to offer a resolution on "pro-life/pro-choice dialogue"? Why was I *surprised* when announcements for P.S. speakers would be ripped down from the bulletin boards on liberal university campuses within minutes of their being posted?

I guess it's because I always assumed that liberals were better. "We," "our type of people," the "progressives," were more tolerant, broad-minded, able to handle conflicts creatively. Or so I'd thought.

(Incidentally, the response of mainstream pro-lifers to our peace-movement proselytism is a wild and oddly symmetrical story—one which will have to be told elsewhere.)

On the other hand, segments of the Christian Left seemed more willing than the secular Left to acknowledge the radiating pain of abortion, and to struggle with it on a moral and pastoral level. Groups like Sojourners, the Catholic Peace Fellowship, Pax Christi, and Evangelicals for Social Action were able to see the surgical invasion of women's wombs and the destruction of our coming-children as a kind of sacrilege. They were also able to regard post-abortion women as veterans of an unjust "war"; agents of violence, but, much more, victims of it.

Even within the more congenial sectors of the Christian Left, talking about abortion was difficult. But as more and more people allowed their ambivalences about abortion to come to the surface—and as those ambivalences escalated to the sticking point—*not* talking about it became impossible.

For a long time most of the "dialogue" or "debate" appeared to be between Catholics and ex-Catholics. Did it only seem that way to me? After all, my home base (Erie, Pennsylvania) was predominantly a parish-and-pizza kind of town; I circulated in the heavily Catholic Northeast and Midwest; and even the other "movements" with which I was involved (United Farm Workers, anti-war, and such) were thick with people coming or going, to or from, Catholicism.

Even beyond the little circles of my own experience, in the larger culture, when *this* was the topic it seemed that being a Catholic or not made a big difference.

Nobody who spoke out for or against abortion was ever identified as an "ex-*Jew*" or a "former *Methodist* seminarian.*"* When they wanted a pro-choice sound-bite, the major media relied heavily on ex-Catholics, post-Catholics, and semi-Catholics—one would think these were the three major religious denominations in America.

In the other camp, it was always the Diocesan Women's Guild and the Knights of Columbus out there collecting maternity clothes for the Pregnancy Aid Center; the State Catholic Conference lobbying against the death penalty, strip-mining, *and abortion;* the klatch of Cardinals up there testifying against funding the MX missile *and abortion.* The Catholics, again.

I wanted dialogue. But where could you find some sort of De-Militarized Zone in the midst of the polarized debate, some common ground where people could get together to open their hearts and receive each other? At the Women's Center? (Ha.)

Where could you hope to find a forum on a consistent—even a coherent—ethic on killing? In the university? (Ha, ha.)

Or where could you get support for women—young women, women with no money—so that they could face an unexpected pregnancy with confidence and dignity? From the medical establishment? Holy Mother the State? (You get the picture.)

Faulty as it was, the Church was the only game in town.

And it goes beyond the Church as an organizing tool or an institutional base for ministry. It dawned on me that, precisely at their most dogmatic, this Church's teachings *are* consistently against murder, whether by the bomb, abortion, or a baseball bat. It was not Right Wing or Left Wing. I grasped that when this consistency is obscured, it is the fault not of the dogma but of teachers who fail to teach the Whole Thing: teachers who have assimilated to the culture, who have sold out left and right.

So after orbiting the Church for a long time, I came in, finally, for a landing.

Was it all an intellectual thing? No. The Church gave me a coherent ethical position on life-and-death questions, for which I was grateful; but, much more than that, the Church is a community with the heart of Jesus at heart.

Before, I had been troubled with the identification I'd felt with that undocumented alien, the shrimp-sized embryo: I'd thought it was incompatible with solidarity with women. Now, I saw, with a flow of wonder, the identification of God Almighty with the embryo. I saw also the outpouring of the Spirit on women, slaves and Gentiles, and children, born and unborn, as a revelation: don't cut us apart! We are one!

I saw the significance of a Mary-like soul, a Mary-like Church, and a Mary-like Cosmos, which could receive the Word of God and keep it, grow it, and bring it to birth. (Now *there's* a womanistic theme to be found in this putatively patriarchal Church!) I loved the poetry *and* the dogmatics; I loved the tenderness of the tradition.

I loved it not only because it was beautiful. Anyone (at least, anyone as bright as most of my friends) could think up a half a dozen beautiful myths in the course of a morning spirituality workshop, and concoct a sacrament or two over lunch. No, I loved the Catholic tradition because it is actually true.

So it was a whiff of the sea, a shoreline testing of the water, and then a headlong dive back into the depths of the notorious pro-life Church, the *Pacem in Terris* Church, the old Church which had out-lived everything, even my skepticism.

Was it all so heady and romantic and overheated? And did I end up running with a pack of *awful* triumphalistic popish anti-choice fanatics? No. There was a lot of work to be done, the great Yes and No: No to the killing and Yes to the living. So my friends and I didn't have that much time to stay totally misty-eyed and mystical about it.

For one thing, we held the Sexual Revolution responsible for too many hurt and too many dead; so we were doing everything we could think of, culturally and personally, to replace the Sexual Revolution with Sexual Shalom. We were trying to restore the traditional Christian vision of natural sex, sacred sex, at the service of the family, and bonding, and life.

This was supposedly "conservative."

On another front, we were also trying to get support for women who were unprovided for at the time of pregnancy—comprehensive "human services" at the political level, mutual aid and advocacy at the street level—so that women would not be subjected to the insecurity and panic which coerced so many into destroying their young. "Support, don't abort"—that was our theme.

This was supposedly "liberal."

We struggled to get the courts and legislatures to recognize that "personhood" is co-extensive with human life, and that human rights begin where human life begins. We tried to win a progressive expansion of recognition of the human rights of everybody without exception.

A very "establishment" way of pursuing a progressive goal.

And we wanted to directly protect pregnant women, and the children they carry, from medical violence. As simple as that. So we organized sit-ins to try to shut down the abortion places, providing the women with another chance to find nonviolent alternatives. This tactic actually saved hundreds of lives; and, as the Talmud says, "To save one life, it is as if you had saved the whole world."

A radical way of pursuing a very traditional goal.

The labels came to mean less as the reality of our work meant more.

I married a Baptist I met during a sit-in campaign and had a baby, finally, at age thirty-eight (my favorite pro-life direct action, by the way). It gave me to understand in the flesh the honorable and enduring love of a man, and the dearness of ties to women (like the St. Mary's Morning Mass ladies who took me under their wings: yes, I liked being clucked over!). I understood better the vulnerability of the birth-giving woman, and the incredible power which flows through her.

Shalom: we used to say it was "from the cradle to the grave," but of course it doesn't begin at the *cradle;* "from womb to tomb"? But it doesn't end at the *tomb.*

Now I say Shalom is "from erection to resurrection." It's acting in the benevolence of God, under the Mercy, excluding nobody, please God, and holding even the littlest ones dear.

4

The Daughters of Heaven Are Weeping

Colleen C. Conant

Colleen C. Conant is managing editor of *The Commercial Appeal* in Memphis. She majored in music and minored in religion and philosophy at Oklahoma City University. She was greatly influenced by her college experience in the 1960s, where freedom of expression and exploration of ideas were encouraged. She is embarking upon her third decade in the field of journalism. An active Episcopal laywoman, she serves on the editorial board of *The Church News*.

My darling sons:

You are so young and bright and full of the promise of life. Your energy level will not tolerate a quiet discussion of weighty issues.

Yet the world is tilting as it turns these days, in part because of this troubling issue of abortion.

It is not a matter of concern for you now, but it will push itself into your lives some day. Perhaps you will be ready, more ready than I was, but if you are not, I'd like to think that I offered some level of comfort as you wrestle with your convictions.

You are young men. You are white, Anglo-Saxon. By this accident of race and gender you have inherited the earth. You will never face the oppression of being a minority. You will have the privilege and profound responsibility of influencing the lives of others as you ascend in the world.

In your lifetime, women will begin to more fully share the role of leadership, but men will dominate the seats of power. You will be among them on some plateau. You must be ready. You must be wiser and more tolerant than your father and I. You have the opportunity to forge ahead boldly and lovingly in this difficult issue.

You must come to your own choice in this matter of abortion, as in every matter. But you will come to those choices from the words you will have heard at home and the attitudes you will have adopted from those who love you most.

As you mature you will hear absolutes from people you respect and from strangers. Some of what they all say will be perfectly acceptable to you. A part of growing up is latching on to the ideals and convictions of charismatic leaders. The ultimate maturity is identifying which of those ideals and convictions you really own.

We are a family of faith, my sons. It is the foundation of our home and the rock upon which your father and I established our marriage. We have chosen a church that expresses that faith in inclusive, rather than exclusive, terms. The Episcopal Communion is a tolerant body, rooted in the liturgical traditions of the ancient church. It is a perfect combination for us of order, discipline and openness.

I pray you never will turn away from your faith. Although it may be some slippery, Sunday-school sort of obligation in your life now, that will not always be the case. As you grow and learn, you will begin to own your faith. It will be a precious possession. You will turn to it in all your decisions, frivolous or profound. It will sustain you in moments of confusion and indecision.

Shouting, placard-carrying people on television prompt you to ask me that most basic of questions: Why are those people angry? Then: What does abortion mean? And finally: Why would a mommy not want her baby? Basic, yes, but oh so difficult to answer without imposing my will on you. As I told you earlier, you must come to your own conviction on this matter through faith.

The outspoken in this issue have lined up on opposite sides of a line which separates those who are anti-abortion from those who are pro-choice. They leave little room for a position somewhere in between. In fact, when confronted by leaders of both groups, I have been told that I must choose. There can be no equivocation.

The sacrifice was great when this debate entered the public arena. What each of us gave up was our right to privacy.

I owe you the courtesy of my own thinking and how I have arrived at it. It has not changed over time.

Phrased in the language of the present dialogue I would characterize my position as pro-choice. Let me emphasize that pro-choice can mean choosing not to have an abortion.

Our church teaches that human life is a gift from God to his people and thereby sacred. Your births, my sons, so carefully planned and joyously awaited, underscore that blessing.

Our church also expresses the following with regard to the abortion debate: "Unequivocal opposition to any legislation on the part of national or state governments that would abridge or deny the right of individuals to reach informed decisions in this matter and act upon them."

I believe that no woman who chooses to have an abortion comes to that decision capriciously. I believe abortion is a matter between a woman and God and any other person the woman chooses to bring into the circle. It is absolutely private and not suitable for public debate. I embrace our church's resolution that government must not intrude in this matter.

Why do women have abortions? We cannot know the

heart of every woman who has come to this choice. Nor do we need to. It is private.

Perhaps we would dream of and work for a world where no woman ever would choose to have an abortion. We don't live in that kind of world now. It's not likely we ever will. But I believe it is imperative that the freedom of choice never be abridged.

It is important for you to know that I believe women who have abortions are not evil; they are not murderers as some would characterize them. They are women in personal and private crisis. They are sad, yet resolute.

Remember these daughters of heaven in your prayers.

This is the way they feel . . .

The daughters of heaven are weeping.
   They spill tears of joy for the children of light,
   hushed tears of sorrow for those in the darkness.
   They pray for grace, and rejoice in moments of
      serenity.
   These sisters embrace the absolutes in life.
   They accept consequences in black and white.
   But they live out their lives in shades of gray.
   It is not guilt that torments them. It is grief.

The daughters of heaven are weeping.
   They nurse their babies, their bosom brimful.
   It is a moment precious and private.
   The warm milk flows in rivulets of love.
   The sunlight arouses memories of the others;
   a halo crowns this madonna and child.
   The little ones sleep secure in the sweet folds of
      motherhood and eternity.

This sisterhood does not turn from the choices of life;
even those that are presented randomly.
They ponder what is, what might be, and what never
can be.
Their searching comes from the soul.
A daughter of heaven understands her responsibility:
To God,
to her own body;
she accepts the sanctity of all life;
she steels for the dark moments of difficult decisions.

The daughters of heaven are weeping.
Melancholy invades every maternal moment.
A sister's swollen belly is a silent reminder.
An infant's soft cry is exquisitely sweet.
Tears salt the water of the baptismal font.

The years rush past.
They smile in wonder at the straight, tall children
of light.
In their shadows are the images of those who might
have been,
fair-haired and rosy;
twinkling eyes, long, silky lashes.
A daughter.

The daughters of heaven are weeping.
Their cries accompany the clamor of conflict and
conviction.
Their brothers and sisters take to the streets,
making public this most private reconciliation.
These too are God's children; they care desperately.
They confront and intimidate;

they build public barricades against private resolve.
"Murderers," "Baby killers," the signs proclaim.
Hateful words from loving people.
This public debate is beyond pain for the daughters
     of heaven.
The zooming camera, the strident sound-bite is
     excruciating.
The quiet moments of reverie are wrenching,
 this exhibition is intolerable.

The daughters of heaven are weeping.
 They make their choices in quiet desperation
 or clear, reasoned deliberation.
 They are too young,
 or too old.
 They are sick or world weary.
 They are alone, or
 they have children to feed and clothe and educate.
 They have commitments to loved ones and the
     world.

They walk their chosen path,
never fully free of the grief,
but certain of their course.
The bright eyes of the children of light
lift them up. . . .

Boys, when you grow up you will meet one of these
     daughters of heaven. Perhaps you will love her
     and make a home with her. She will praise God for
     your quiet understanding.

I love you.
Mama

5

And Rachel Wept

Lurlene McDaniel

Lurlene McDaniel has been writing professionally for twenty-three years. Twenty of her novels have been published by Willowisp/School Book Fairs, four titles by Zondervan, and she is working on a series of books for Bantam.

In recent years, her writing has been directed toward the young adult market and has focused on life-altering events such as disease and sibling or parental death. Several of her books are used by health care specialists to help patients adjust to their diagnoses. She teaches regularly at writer's conferences and has created and taught writing courses at Tallahassee Community College and the University of South Florida.

Background: Over twenty million American women have undergone an abortion. Few talk about it openly. Most suffer debilitating effects ranging from guilt to thoughts of suicide, anywhere from one to ten years after the procedure. Clinicians have labeled this phenomenon post-abortion syndrome, seeing similarities between it and the type of behavior experienced by Vietnam veterans years after they have been home from the war.

The millions of unborn dead are gone. And they're in God's hands. But their mothers are in the hands of believers, the Church. How the Church responds to them and their needs will be both a pivotal issue and a sign of its maturity for a generation to come.

Her number is legion. Yet, sitting in the church pews, she looks as normal as everyone else in the congregation. She has a husband and a child, maybe two children. She works hard on the annual rummage sale and the overseas missions committee; she teaches Sunday school, serves in the nursery, and sometimes helps organize fund raisers for the youth group. No one would ever guess how bad she hurts inside. And she doesn't dare tell a soul about the pain that eats at her soul like a cancer.

Her Bible study group would never understand. Neither can she burden the minister with her pain. In fact, if people knew what she'd done, she is certain that they'd be horrified and reject her, perhaps even hate her. She committed a heinous, and in her own mind, an unpardonable sin. She murdered her own child—she had an abortion.

She'd been scared when her pregnancy test had come back positive. So she'd told herself: "It's *my* body. I shouldn't be forced to have a baby." And, after all, the procedure was perfectly legal. Besides, the baby's father didn't want it, and her parents would throw her out if they knew.

The clinic told her it wasn't a real baby—merely "a glob of fetal cells," "a mistake." They could suction it out in a matter of minutes, and her problem would be solved.

Afterwards, she began picking up the pieces of her life. She fell in love, got married, started a family. She was one of the fortunate few. (Statistics show that one in five women who've aborted never conceive again.) Others like her would become pregnant repeatedly and have multiple abortions. But *her* life went on—with one exception. They'd been wrong at the clinic when they'd told her that the abortion would solve her problem. Dead wrong.

There were times when a black depression would blanket her, suffocating other thoughts. On dark days, her mind kept replaying the abortion experience, especially around the anniversary of its occurrence. She could smell the biting, antiseptic odor of the clinic, feel the metal table, cold and hard, against her back. Worst of all, she could hear the mechanical drone of the suction machine as it sucked away the "product of the conception."

Yes, those days were bad; but the nights were worse. She fought nightmares where she dreamed of her unborn baby. She could hear it crying, could hear it calling for her. God, how she longed to hold and comfort it!

In the eighties, when her church got involved with the abortion issue, she filled her days with other church activities, feeling detached and isolated from people in general. At home, she grew irritable and angry. She snapped at her kids, withdrew from her husband, struggled with fatigue and recurring headaches—even wondered if she shouldn't simply end it all.

She prayed about it, begging God to give her peace. The Bible said that he had forgiven her. But every blessing he gave to her seemed like a slap in her face. She didn't deserve *anything*. Not after what she'd done . . .

She didn't know it, but her husband was hurting too. When he'd been in high school and his girlfriend had told him she was pregnant, he'd panicked. How could he go to college if he had to support a wife and child? His girlfriend had told him she wanted an abortion. It seemed like the best solution at the time. And who was he to tell her no? He saw himself as a protector, knew that he'd fight for what was his. But an unborn baby? Well . . . it was *hers.*

He didn't go to the clinic with his girlfriend the morning the procedure was done, just waited by the phone until she called to say, "It's over." She even mailed him a receipt marked "Paid." Months later, they'd gone their separate ways, reaffirming his initial reaction that they'd done the "right thing," even though he felt creepy about the whole business. Eventually he'd married, and now he had children. He'd put the experience out of his mind for years, but lately his thoughts kept returning to that other baby.

Was it a boy or a girl? Would he or she have been smart? Athletic? Perhaps a musical prodigy?

He felt despondent and helpless. Most of all, he felt guilty.

When his church became involved with the abortion debate and with Operation Rescue, by picketing a local abortion clinic, the most he could bring himself to do was write letters to legislators. And truthfully, even that made him extremely uncomfortable—it was a little like the pot calling the kettle black.

He desperately needed to talk to someone, to tell his side of the story. But who? His wife? His boss? His minister? What would they think of him? How could anyone forgive him after what he'd done?

Casualties of War

The abortion battle has left the Church with untold casualties. Not only are unborn babies victims (some estimates set today's worldwide abortion figure at *60 billion*), but also their parents—the women and men who chose to abort them. If God has indeed written his law upon our hearts, and if his presence is evident in his creation, then humanity is without excuse for not knowing him. It shouldn't be surprising, then, that women who've aborted feel a deep, strangulating guilt. (In one test group, of the 72 percent of the women who professed *no belief in God*, 96 percent claimed they regarded abortion as *murder* after having their abortions!) Rationalizing ("I had no other choice at the time"), repressing ("I breezed through the experience—why, I hardly remember it"), and compensating

("If I work hard enough for Jesus, I can make up for it") are manifestations of this guilt.

Frequently, it's the secular realm that jumps on an issue, offering succor and answers. However, unfortunately, pro-choice advocates refuse to acknowledge the gut-wrenching, soul-destroying effects of this guilt labeled post-abortion syndrome. Instead they ignore aborted women's real psychological responses to physical *and* spiritual trauma. Yet given the position that abortion is a harmless, legal, perfectly acceptable action to an unwanted pregnancy, what else can pro-choicers do?

For to recognize PAS means to recognize that abortion is *not* simply a matter of a woman's right to call the shots for her own body. To accept women verbalizing guilt and shame, along with feelings of being victimized, means that morality matters. It means that those "globs of fetal cells," those "mistakes," are real human beings. And it means that aborting them is murder. Therefore, without a mind-set that thinks God's thoughts, what chance for healing does the post-abortal woman have in her hands?

One thing is certain: ignoring the problem doesn't make it go away. Every woman trapped in this vicious snare is one of the "walking wounded," one of those aching souls seeking forgiveness and acceptance. And for the Christian woman, it's especially difficult. She desires to integrate into an evangelical mainstream that often has neither the understanding nor the compassion for the burden she bears.

Jesus healed with the Word and by the laying on of hands. He is the Head, and we, the Church, are his Body. Thus, it becomes our responsibility to minister healing and reconciliation. We believers are called to reach out to these hurting men and women, these victims of spiritual warfare, and to offer what Christ has always offered—new Life.

For the woman who has aborted, it means recognizing and accepting the responsibility for the abortion. It means helping her confront powerful negative feelings that she may have been repressing for years—without added condemnation and guilt. It means helping her abandon anger and bitterness toward herself and others involved in her abortion experience.

The fulfillment of Jeremiah's prophecy about Herod's slaughter of Jewish children is chronicled in Matthew 2: "In Rama was there a voice heard, lamentation, and weeping, and great mourning, Rachel weeping for her children, and would not be comforted, because they are not."

Today these poignant and eloquent words reach across the centuries with fresh meaning. The woman who has aborted must grieve, must mourn, for her unborn children. The man who watched and waited while his yet-to-be-born child died, must be allowed to mourn as well. One woman told me: "My son's kitten died and we had a funeral for it in the back yard. I watched his tear-stained face as he lowered the box that held his pet into the ground and felt a huge lump inside my throat. And then it occurred to me that I was shedding tears over a dead animal . . . a creature without a soul. Years before, I'd had an abortion and never in all this time had I consciously thought about that unborn baby. I'd never cried for it, or about it. The revelation shook me so profoundly that I started to cry and I couldn't stop. My son kept asking, 'What's wrong, Mommy?' And I couldn't tell him."

For the Church, helping all those suffering from PAS means listening with nonjudgmental ears; it also means hearing with empathetic and compassionate hearts. It usually means public recognition and a proclamation of forgiveness from the pulpit. Matthew 10:8 tells us: "Freely ye have received, freely give." Additionally, a congregation needs to know where its leadership stands before it can "go and do likewise." The post-abortal woman sitting in the pews needs to know that she'll be received with the same amount of compassion given to confessing alcoholics or drug addicts or former convicts.

Education is another fundamental key to opening up this issue. At its very best, it may mean a counseling program sponsored by a church with trained, qualified people who've walked down this road themselves. Our attitude cannot be like that of the parishioner who said: "It was their choice and they made the wrong one. They're getting exactly what they deserve." If it is, we will have failed miserably.

Education linked with Bible studies is especially healing. Because there is power in the Word and because the Word convicts, it can enlighten and minister more than a hundred worldly psychologists. In fact, because forgiveness is such a key factor in this syndrome, *only* the church has the answer for these women, because only the Church can offer Christ. And it is only Christ who freely gives the assurance of what the Greeks called *zoe*—eternal life—the very essence of God himself. With this comes the hope and the promise that one day all believers will be together in paradise—

and that a woman, once there, will be reunited with her aborted child.

It is this spiritual dimension, this understanding that the abortion battle is not simply political or social or cultural, that gives the war its absolute focus and its deadly seriousness. The Kingdom of Light battles the Kingdom of Darkness. And as Paul pointed out to the believers at Ephesus, "We wrestle not against flesh and blood, but against principalities, against powers, against the rulers of the darkness of this world, against spiritual wickedness in high places."

Regardless of how long the battle rages here on earth, the victory is God's. It is my hope, my confidence, that in retrospect, future generations will remember this as one of Christendom's finest hours. Not one of civil war and divided camps. Not one of ducking the abortion issue because it's too hot. But one of reaching out to those who had no voice—or had voices too afraid, too ashamed to speak.

Let it be a journey from "a time to weep" to a "time to laugh." A voyage from a "time to mourn" to a "time to dance." For all the unborn babies. For all the weeping Rachels.

6

A Faith-Filled Talk of Life and Death

Judy Mathe Foley

Judy Mathe Foley is a freelance writer and editor who lives in Philadelphia. For twenty-two years she was managing editor of *The Episcopalian,* the national magazine of the Episcopal Church. She has participated in the legislative battle for abortion rights since before *Roe v. Wade.* She believes that the public debate over abortion will be settled with the introduction into the United States of RU485 and that her grandchildren will need to know a great deal about how to make moral decisions.

Put down your placard that says "Stop the Baby Killers," and I'll put down mine that says "Keep Your Laws Off My Body," and let's have a faith-filled talk of life and death, subjects that can't be contained on picket line posters and prescribed in slogans.

Too often a "religious discussion" about abortion concerns whether life begins at birth and whether "Thou shalt not kill" applies to a fetus. But let's not limit ourselves to legality which is cold and controlling and narrowly prescribes the debate in unequivocal statements such as "Abortion is murder" and "A woman has the right to control her body." Man-made doctrinal interpretations turn into "So's-your-old-man!" exercises, and biblical textproofing gets boring and repetitious.

Instead, let's have the courage to move onto more treacherous ground, into a place a friend of mine calls "the fuzzy edges." Let's see what we can discern of our faith and how it applies to decision-making about the whole of life. We can do so with the assurance of the all-important Christian element of grace—we can be forgiven. We may be wrong, but we will not be condemned for our groping.

We don't have a "right" to life or a "right" to reproductive freedom. We have only real-life ambiguities. All of God's creation can't be contained on a picket sign or codified into law. If that were true, we wouldn't need anything else but the Ten Commandments, and the Bible would have ended when Moses came down off the mountain with the tablets.

Instead, God sent his Son to give us on-the-job training in how to live in this miraculous place we've been given. And he left us a manual, illustrated with examples, of his decision-making method. The Gospel parables are filled with all the maddening ambiguity God unleashed when he gave each of us the power to reason.

Take, for example, the parable of the prodigal son. A land-rich father divides his estate between his two sons. The loyal, elder son stays home to work in his father's fields. As children trying to find their own lives are wont to do, whether in fourth-century Palestine or twentieth-century USA, the younger son goes adventuring in a distant country, squanders his inheritance, and is destitute.

He comes home repentant and asks if he can work as a hired hand. Instead, the overjoyed father throws him a welcome-home party! The older son, cut to the quick by this show of paternal love for his irresponsible sibling, says, "But, Dad, I've stayed here and helped you all these years and you never gave me a party. You never even killed a goat for me. But *he* comes home and you kill a fatted calf."

"Yes, I know you've been loyal, and for that loyalty I've given you your inheritance," the father answers. "But my other son needs me now because he's had a hard time. Now that he's safely home, we must celebrate."

What's going on here? Didn't we already have the law that tells us to "honor thy father and thy mother"? Wasn't that the law on which the elder son was operating? So what's Jesus doing telling this story which rewards the profligate son? Any parent knows the answer. Sometimes parents need more than a set of safe rules if they are going to raise inquisitive, healthy children who will grow into adults capable of making decisions for themselves.

In parenting, as in most of life, a pre-packaged, one-size-fits-all rule seldom solves problems and rarely allows any room to grow. Life is more complex than that. Laws are only for the bad times, tools to settle disputes when all else fails. For instance, the law, as stated in the deed to the city rowhouse my husband and I own, says we control the 25-foot wide strip of our backyard and our next-door neighbor owns the adjoining 25-foot strip. The fence that runs down the middle separates our legal responsibilities.

In the best of times, when we enjoy our neighbors, we can be scofflaws. We can regularly break the law. We can tear down the fence and share the 50-foot space with our neighbor. Only when we disagree do we need to revert to the law to separate out what belongs to whom. And even the very existence of the legal proof of possession is no instant panacea. We will still have to wrestle with decisions. Should we sue? If we sue, will we lose a friendship? Is the temporary satisfaction we might feel from winning a lawsuit worth creating a nasty neighborhood situation? If we don't sue, but find no other solution, will we feel victimized?

Now it would be reassuring to be able to make a once-and-future judgment call. Say this is it, life begins at conception, thou shalt not kill, abortion is killing. Wrap that up into a law that says abortion is murder and murder is illegal, chalk it up on the law books, rub our hands together and say "Well, we've handled that, and it feels good."

Suppose Jesus were to meet a twentieth-century woman who works every available overtime she can in a hospital emergency room at night and goes to nursing school during the day the whole time her teenage daughter and son are in high school. She often feels guilty about not spending more time with them, but they are cooperative and loving. Now, just as they are about to become the first in her family ever to go to college, she finds herself pregnant. Knowing she will not be able to meet tuition payments if she must care for another child, and unable to bear the thought of telling them that what they've all worked for so long just can't be, she has an abortion. Would the Jesus of the parables automatically condemn her? Would he quote a law prohibiting "abortions of convenience"?

When a man too sick to get to healing waters approached Jesus on the Sabbath, a day on which Jewish law prohibited doing any work, did the Son of God say, "Sorry, today's my day off. Take two aspirins and call my office on Monday"?

That image of Jesus jars, not just because it's so far from the way he would act, but because it is taken out of the vineyards and grain fields where his parables were taught. We've lost more than we realize by the fact that we no longer live in an agrarian society. Styrofoam and plastic separate us from other living, growing things. We've lost the voice of the farmer, the person who knows life-and-death processes firsthand and understands the relationship between the two. In conversations about abortion and death and killing, we've lost sight of the fact that life is more than birth and no less than death.

Birth, though a truly miraculous process, is only one

of many miracles in God's world over which we have stewardship. Sometimes that stewardship will involve making choices because we are co-creators with God of a constantly evolving creation. Every decision we make cuts off another road—that's the unfortunate nature of decision-making! And even when decisions turn out happily, each road not taken can cause regret.

In his book *The Lively Experiment,* which recounts the beginnings of religious freedom in the newly forming United States, Episcopal historian Sidney Mead writes compellingly of how the Native Americans, who lived in tune with nature, were wiped out by settlers who, by necessity of survival, "had no time for remorse but only time for the labor in the cold and in the heat and in the vast places."

Mead quotes a poignant observation of Francis Parkman. While hunting for food on the Oregon Trail, he shot an antelope. "When I stood by his side, the antelope turned his expiring eye upward. It was like a beautiful woman's, dark and bright. 'Fortunate that I am in a hurry,' thought I; 'I might be troubled with remorse, if I had time for it.' "

In my small city garden are wild, velvety purple and translucently pink morning glories, such lushly beautiful blooms that, though they climb my iris and choke my roses, I cannot bring myself to pull them out (my husband has no such compunction when they strangle his snap beans!). I've "given them life" by not *destroying* them as seedlings, but they are an ungrateful and obstreperous lot! I have to enjoy them on their own terms. They show their brilliant hues only in the morning—when I'm at other tasks and rarely in the garden—and I cannot possess them by bringing them into the house, because they wither away as soon as I cut them from their vines.

Parenting, like gardening, requires some of the same hands-off treatment, and the stakes are so much higher with a reasoning human being whose life is so much longer than the short summer of a morning glory. At some point when our son was a toddler, I realized we were the only parents he would ever have—an awesome responsibility on which the future literally depends. Are we not at our most responsible and our most faithful when we follow Jesus' example and question not only our laws, but our hearts, when we consider not only whether to bring children into the world, but what kind of world we'll bring them into?

The message of Jesus' parables is not that he came to make decisions for us, but that he came to teach us how to use our resources to make them ourselves. And we could have no better guide. As one of my favorite teachers, the English theologian Dorothy Sayers, has written: "Perhaps it is no wonder that the women were first at the Cradle and last at the Cross. They had never known a man like this Man—there never has been such another. A prophet and teacher who never nagged at them, never flattered or coaxed or patronized . . . who rebuked without querulousness and praised without condescension, who took their questions and arguments seriously, who never mapped out their sphere for them."

Life is a journey, not a destination. Not a commute, but a slow Sunday drive through God's creation. We would do well to observe it carefully and learn from its rhythms where our real responsibility as stewards lies.

7

A Bishop's Letter to Her Goddaughter

Bishop Judith Craig

Judith Craig is bishop of the Michigan Area of the United Methodist Church. She previously served as council director, Conference Council on Ministries, and held a pastorate and an associate pastorate in the East Ohio Conference. She holds a master of divinity degree from Union Theological Seminary in New York and has done postgraduate work in the religious education of adults at Teachers College, Union and Columbia University, New York.

Dear Kirsten:

Today you heard the tape recording of a heartbeat in your mother's womb! That heartbeat will, we hope, become the life beat of your little brother or sister. Today you heard the heartbeat when the life in your mother was only three and a half months old. How exciting! I wonder if by the time you are thirty such a wonder will have become "old hat" and there will be new wonders to enjoy if you are carrying a child forming in your womb. This carrying of life inside another is truly one of God's most mysterious miracles. To hear the heartbeat as you have in 1990 is wondrous. I hope it will still be wondrous to you in 2020.

It was your grandmother who told me about the tape recording. She was so excited, and talked about how your mother was all aglow with the reality hearing it brought home to her. Because your mother has been like a daughter to me, and you like a grandchild, I was excited too. Your people are family to me; and I enjoy, with all of you, the anticipation of that new life as if it were to be my own grandchild . . . the way I enjoy you!

That sound of a heartbeat at fourteen weeks was, for your mom, a source of incredible joy and anticipation. For you it as probably puzzling—you are only two—but I am so grateful for our late twentieth-century technology that gives us such moments.

I smile to myself and thank God for this miracle. I imagine your mom and dad listening with loving delight to the sound of a life forming, a life rising out of their loving intention and readiness to take that little life into the circle of your family. There, your sister or brother will know the same ready acceptance and nurture you are enjoying now. The future will be open and inviting for all of you as that life becomes part of your daily life.

And then I remember it is not always so for life forming in a womb. The moment of conception is miraculous in its placement in God's life plan. But the circumstances surrounding that moment, the coming together of male and female that spawns conception, is not always a moment of living intention and integrity and mutual desire for intimacy. I remember another young woman finding herself with the awareness of a fetus stirring within her, moving toward life as a child. But this fetus was the result of violence and terror. She was raped. I remember the sound of her voice and the look in her eyes and the confusion let loose in her life as she and her fiance came seeking counsel from her pastor. She was pregnant from a rape that had frightened her so much that she had not reported it. Only six weeks later I was to marry that couple now sitting with me seeking counsel. What should they do? What should she do?

As I think about your tape of the heartbeat, I wonder what the sound of a fetal heartbeat would have meant to that young woman and her fiance? For your parents and grandparents, that sound was wondrous, evoking smiles and pleasant anticipation. For that other young woman, I think the heartbeat would have evoked the fear and terror of an act of violent assault that left her feeling only repugnance for anything that reminded her of it. Should she and her fiance begin their marriage with the reality of her night of terror as the central heartbeat of their life together?

I counseled that they should not. So did the physician we contacted. This was before the Supreme Court case called *Roe v. Wade*. It was difficult to find a place where a safe and legal abortion could be done. The doctor helped us. It was done. I still know that young couple well, and I think they still believe with me that we made the right choice in those days. It was not easy for any of us. There was an emerging life in her womb. Should we interrupt that development? What was our obligation to that emerging life, whose origin was violence and terror, as compared to obligation to two lives about to become one in loving, committed, faithful intention?

Fetal heartbeats. Emerging life in the womb of woman. Excruciating decisions about the life of a woman and the life of a child forming. I write this letter in a time when people of conscience are being torn and tested by whether or not we should as a society continue to make the possibility of interrupting fetal life legal. For some, this is an all-consuming issue. It has become one of the central lenses through which our morality is examined. With every marvelous advance of medicine and the ability to sustain younger and younger life to full maturity outside the womb, the conundrum intensifies. Now persons of faith, seeking to weigh the issues in faith forums, are joined by judges and legislators and public opinion influencers in the search for "right" and "truth" and "the will of God" concerning abortion. Is it ever right? Is it never right? Who should decide? How should they decide?

The times are awhirl with those who take strong stands and those who want to take no stand at all. In the midst of the controversy I find persons who tell me they have prayed their way to absolute certainty about it, while others tell me of their equally earnest prayers that leave them less ready to be absolutely sure about every case in every circumstance. I am in the latter group. I am clear about The United Methodist Church's stated position that abortion is not to be used as a casual means of birth control, or for other personal gratifications such as sex selection or genetic engineering. I agree that only in the most tragic conflicts of life can abortion be acceptable. Even then there is grief and lingering pain only God's mercy can heal. And, I believe that decision can be reached only after the most thoughtful, prayerful counsel has been given and the wisest medical advice secured.

The woman whose body carries that emerging life must be at the center of the decision, but she should surround herself with those who can give wise counsel, and the others in primary relationship to her and that emerging life, including the father if possible. When those conditions are met, and there is clearly more possibility of disruption of life for that woman and others around her than there is hope of healthy and wholesome journey through pregnancy, delivery, and lifelong care for the child that is to be, then I believe one can, in God's mercy, undertake an abortion. The faithful testing of all those factors will limit those times, and the counsel may sometimes lead to decisions to carry a life to full development, give it birth, and place it in another's care for the nurture a natural mother may not be able to provide.

What is important to me is that the legal and safe means for that choice be maintained. I stand in opposition to legislative and judicial actions that draw legal restrictions so tightly as to disable the possibility of making that agonizing choice. Therefore, I am opposed to a repeal of the Supreme Court's decision on *Roe v. Wade*. I am opposed to a constitutional amendment banning abortion. I am opposed to laws that remove what is legal from the reach of some, especially the poor, by saying some medical plans will pay for this legal procedure but some will not. I am opposed to approaching what I believe to be a moral and ethical decision by writing sweeping laws that put every man, woman, child, and developing fetus into one category for judgment. Such legislative action results in indiscriminate denial of the variety of human circumstance and becomes discriminatory intrusion into one of the most private moments of decision in the human life span.

Kirsten, I want you to know that as I write this in 1990 I cannot tolerate cavalier, unthinking, selfish, convenient, hasty use of abortion as a means of birth control. At the same time, I resist the intrusion of legislative and judicial policy into a realm I believe to be intimately personal, deeply moral, and properly defined as private.

For that I am accused of being "pro choice" by those who call themselves "pro life." It stings. Am I, then, "anti life"? No! I, too, am pro life if that means "for life." I want to preserve compassion and human dignity in decisions that require agonizing search for God's merciful guidance. I am pro life. I abhor violence against emerging life, against young life that cannot protect itself, against adult life misused and abused. I am pro life. I want gun control laws to make firearms less accessible in moments of heat and anger. I hope for even more destruction of war weapons and signing of peace treaties. I am pro life. I join those who seek to find ways to distribute food and means of shelter more equitably among the peoples of the world.

But because I do not view all pregnant women as if their circumstances are the same, I am called "pro choice" as antithesis to "pro life." Because I want to maintain the right of women to make critical choices about their own future and what might be the future of potential life within them, I am called "pro choice" with the implication of being against life. I share that demeaning labeling with others who hold similar positions in the midst of the controversy. I share the appellation, the charge, the accusation with some wonderfully brave people who are much more vocal and visible than I am. And I receive the label from equally wonderful and brave people with whom I would choose to be allies if there were some way to bridge the chasm opened by the insistently separating way this controversy is cast in our time.

But the cruelest, crudest expression of disdain for my conviction that we must preserve the right of choice for women comes in the form of letters that call me a "baby killer." Even more painful is the fact that those letters are written by children eight, nine, ten years old. They ask me how a bishop can want to kill babies. Have I not taken Jesus into my heart? asked one. Can I be a Christian and want to kill babies? Those letters cut me to the quick. It is not just the attack on me that is distressing. I am hurt that adults, people of conscience themselves, would use children in what appears to be a way to get at me. Do those adults not understand that aside from painting false pictures for their children, they are also subtly undermining their children's confidence in the church by attacking those who hold visible and sacred office in it? What kind of care for children is it when we take public persons and misrepresent their intentions in the minds of those children?

Kirsten, I write this now with little ability to imagine life as you will know it in the early twenty-first century. You will enjoy wonders and possibilities I cannot foresee. I have confidence some of the emerging knowledge about ways we can live creatively on our planet will have taken root and be bearing fruit of concord and well-being for your generation. Whatever else is happening, I am confident one miracle will still be occurring. There will be the miracle of life rising out of loving intimacy between a man and a woman. There will be constellations of parent-children that will know the joys and wonders of life cycles I watch and enjoy now. The Christian will still hold a basic conviction that all life is sacred. It is a trust from God given us to nurture and tend with intention for goodness and loving respect. As I struggle with whether or not anyone should practice abortion, I do it standing on that conviction. Whatever people may think of me or say about me, I hope they will know and respect my basic reverence for life. I hope you share that reverence all the years of your life.

There reside in me several longings in the midst of this late twentieth-century controversy. I long for a way for those who oppose each other to exhibit reverence for each other's lives. So much of the speechmaking and public demonstration is violent and disrespectful of the human dignity of the opposition. When discussing matters of life preservation I hope we make evident our mutual respect.

I long for women's voices to be taken seriously. Men are indeed involved in the act of procreation, but for men to be deciding for women whose circumstances they do not know and cannot imagine, without careful hearing of women's agony and plea for their own lives and well-being, is like denying the value of women. It is a human issue we are discussing. I want the fullness of human experience, male and female, to be brought to bear.

I long for deliverance from having this one issue become the measuring rod for the totality of one's moral and ethical thought. How tragic when all the rest of one's ethics and morality is questioned or affirmed based on this one element of a much broader set of responsible and faithful consciousness. The claim that one's whole moral stance can be discerned according to the position taken on any one issue is a denial of the breadth and depth of another human being's integrity.

I long to be able to speak openly about my personal search for truth and wisdom in this matter without evoking in the minds of those who disagree with me a disrespect for the office I am privileged to hold. I recognize that I must take care lest my personal opinion be announced in a way that cloaks it in the office of bishop. What I regret is when my personal thought is denied expression because others will impugn the office if they disagree with the person holding that office.

All of that means that I long for the persons in opposition to each other on the issue of abortion to wage their disagreement in ways that do not become assaults on life. Violent public demonstration, intrusion into moments of personal agony, the hurling of epithets, the display of dehumanizing placards, the disagreement with ideas becoming an attack on personal integrity are all behaviors that are tearing person from person, community from community. That very result is itself a tragic conflict of life with life, and in the very moment we are searching for ways to sustain the quality of life as reverence, we use irreverent and destructive means. How sad and contradictory that seems to me!

I cannot tell you what counsel I would offer any woman who might come to me today considering abortion. We would have to search out all the surrounding circumstances that bring her to the moment. Is there violence? Is there illness? Is there threat to other life brought by the emerging life? Is there intentional and compassionate selfless love ready to receive life? Is this a matter of convenience or urgent conflict of life with life? I would have to surround that conversation with the awareness of how many women there are who ache to hear the sound of a heartbeat in their womb and cannot and would welcome a newborn life into their realm of care. So many factors to consider, so much information to gather, so earnest a prayer time to enter before a counsel can be mutually offered by seeker and sought.

But this I can tell you, Kirsten. I want a safe, legal option for any woman who might come to me, any woman anywhere, regardless of her social status or economic means. I want the choice to remain open, even as I want it to be exercised only under the most difficult of circumstances. I want the careful and medically sound possibility available even though I know its use will always carry wounding and difficult memory for those who choose it, whatever the clarity or confusion of their choice. I want every woman to be free of taunting and accusation and judgment by those who cannot possibly know her reality. And I want her reality tested in a circle of wise and prayerful counsel.

I cannot see into your future, Kirsten. I can celebrate that you are and that your parents take such delight in you and their love that they want to bring into being yet more life. I depend on God's grace to continue to sustain you and your family. I thank God for the precious gift of life you and all children are. Perhaps by the time you are an adult, your generation will have learned more humane and helpful ways to work through controversies of moral and ethical choice than my generation is employing. I hope so, for I want to leave you a legacy of reverence for life and joyful anticipation of its creation.

Bishop Judith Craig
Michigan Area
The United Methodist Church

8

Seed Corn Must Not Be Ground

Marilou Awiakta

Marilou Awiakta is a Cherokee-Appalachian poet and author. In 1986, the United States Information Agency chose her books, *Abiding Appalachia: Where Mountain and Atom Meet* and *Rising Fawn and the Fire Mystery* (St. Luke's Press) for the global tour of its show "Women in the Contemporary World." Through Tufts University, she is currently working with a network of eighty scholars to "develop a new model of American studies, using black, ethnic and feminist perspectives to integrate the sciences and humanities." She was honored with a Distinguished Writer award in 1989.

The gender that bears life must not be separated from the power to sustain it: This is the Creator's law for the survival of all warm-blooded species, including the human. Traditionally, American Indians have woven this law into their cultures. In its abortion ruling, the U.S. Supreme Court has set the stage for the separation of the issue of birth from the issue of nurture, thereby separating woman from the power of choice and from the power to sustain the life she bears. This ruling is not compatible with the survival of the people. I am working in all possible ways to restore the wisdom of the Creator's law.

I remember the story of my Cherokee foremothers, known collectively as "the Grandmothers." That's why the U. S. Supreme Court's decision on abortion is a rock hurled through the web of my life and through the greater web of which mine is a part. A radial strand—the Creator's law of survival—is severed. Women are being separated from the power to sustain the life we bear. Reverberating with the impact, the whole web sags slightly. I am stunned. As a mother and a woman of faith, I cannot let the web go unmended. But what can I do?

First, I am still, listening to messages that vibrate along intact strands. From a radial one reaching beyond my life into the past comes the voice of the Grandmothers—strong women who, like their other American Indian sisters, lived in cultures that abided by the Creator's laws and held the welfare of children paramount. The Supreme Court has confined its decision to birth alone—the production of children. But the Grandmothers say, "Who will take care of the children? Who will feed, clothe, shelter, educate, protect—nurture them to maturity?" They insist, and so do I, that the issue of children's care must be resolved before the issue of birth is even considered. To do otherwise is unconscionable. "Children are the seeds of the people. Seed corn must not be ground," is the ancient tribal wisdom for survival.

In my own city, I show the Grandmothers a microcosm of the "grinding of children" that is a national disgrace: physical and sexual abuse, economic exploitation through drugs and the sex industry, the steady descent of women and children into poverty, the violence toward women of all ages. "Although we've had the vote for 65 years," I explain, "until recently women have been barred from policy-making bodies that govern life in America. Even now, on a national level, our power is weak: one in nine on the Supreme Court, four percent in the Congress and about the same in the state legislatures. We do not have equal representation in making any laws, not even in this abortion decision that controls our own bodies. We are being undermined, disenfranchised, disempowered. . . ."

Calm and steady, the Grandmothers have listened intently. "We've heard this story before. Remember what happened then to the people . . ."

I do remember. I'd thought it would never come to this—again. Seemingly, the Women's Movement was mending the Creator's law that was broken in the Grandmothers' time. I'd thought my daughters—and surely my granddaughters—would serve with men on the councils of the land, resuming their ancestors' place as "Mothers of the Nation." I'd thought they and my son and their children would live in a society restored to the balance that ensures survival. . . .

"Seed corn must not be ground." What can I do? I am a poet, a writer. I have no political clout, no big money to roll. But I do have faith in the Creator. And I do remember the Grandmothers' story. I must *tell* it to my children, for it has been erased from most books. Hearing it, they will better understand the Web of Life and their places in it. Science teaches them the web's pattern, but not that the laws holding it in place are sacred. The story will also help my children realize how crucial it is to keep any issue within its context when making a decision. An issue, too, is part of a web.

In this abortion controversy, which will reverberate into their lives, I want my descendants to know that in my time of 1990, I remember the role of the Grandmothers: "Family first—and that includes all my people." I remember the principle from the Great Law of Peace of our Iroquois cousins: "In all our deliberations, we must consider the effects of our decisions on the next seven generations." Although I live in a society geared to technology and governed by law based on property, I pull the strength of my mothers—from my own mother to the ancestors—around me like a shawl, and tell the story.

It begins with the Creator's laws, which my family—all United Methodists—taught me Jesus came to fulfill. "In all his teachings," they said, "Jesus shows us how to live in harmony with these laws—and that includes his restoration of women as persons of worth and judgment." Like my grandfather, who was an ordained minister, my parents used a real spider's web, one I could see and touch, to teach me. I pass on some of what I learned . . .

The Creator made the Web of Life and into each strand put the law to govern it. Everything in the universe is part of the web. Stars, trees, oceans, creatures, humans, stones: we are all related. One family. What happens to one will happen to all, for the Creator's laws function this way. They teach us to cooperate and live in harmony, in balance. Ignorance of the laws is no excuse, because through Mother Earth the Creator reveals them continually. If we are reverent toward her and take only what we need, she will sustain us. If we are irreverent and take too much, we separate ourselves from her power and we will die.

A similar law governs all warm-blooded species, including the human. The gender that bears life must not be separated from the power to sustain it. From the eagle to the mouse, from the bear to the whale, the female has the power to nurture and protect her young. A complementary law governs the siring gender, who ranges farther and is more changeable and transitory. Together, the laws make a balance which provides for continuance in the midst of change—and for the survival of the species.

For centuries American Indians studied the Creator's web and wove the sacred laws into their own cultures, each tribe according to its customs. The story of the Cherokee Grandmothers shows how the people interpreted the law for the female—making the welfare of children paramount—and of what happened when that law was broken.

Cherokee women were the center of the family and the center of the Nation, which at its zenith included parts of eight Southern states. The people were divided into seven Mother Clans, with descent—legitimacy—through the mother, for "the womb cannot lie." In marriage, the husband and children took the name of the mother's clan. In divorce, which either partner could initiate, the name, house, children stayed with the mother. Women trained the chiefs and had equal power with men in the council. If the nation considered war, women had a strong say, for they bore the warriors. Sometimes they went into battle with their husband and sons. Abuse of women and children was anathema, for the Cherokee considered it suicidal to damage their life-force.

During menses, a sacred state when their power sign was at its highest, women withdrew for meditation and rest. The Creator having provided roots and herbs for birth control, family planning was left to the women, who did the work of bearing and much of the child care. Like men, women were healers and spiritual leaders. It was believed that the Beloved Woman, chief of the women's council, often brought messages from the Creator to the people.

Life had been going on this way for about two thousand years when the European men first arrived. The Cherokee men asked, "Where are your women?"

And the Europeans said, "What are your women doing here?" To their minds, it was "pagan" and "uncivilized" to have women in places of power. Besides, the Europeans followed the laws of property. And the property they wanted was the land. To get it, it was evident they would have to upset the tribal

95

balance. A primary way to do that was to undermine the power of the women. No rocks at first. Just steady pressure for decades. They refused to deal with women in treaty negotiations. They called the Cherokee system a "petticoat government" and insisted on their own way. They introduced alcohol to the people. And within the wholesome teachings of Christianity, which the Cherokee found familiar and sound—God is Creator of all; love God, and your neighbor as yourself—many missionaries also brought the concept that woman is unclean (because of menses) and the cause of the fall of man. This teaching alarmed the people, for it was well known that "a people cannot be conquered until the hearts of its women are on the ground." Meanwhile, on diplomatic and military levels, the men fought losing battles. Word came back along the great trade routes that the process was everywhere the same in Indian country.

But there was hopeful news from the Iroquois in the North. As a primary model for their constitution, Benjamin Franklin and his colleagues were studying the League of the Iroquois and its Great Law of Peace, which by the late 1700s had united five, then six nations for centuries. Based on equal representation and balance of power, the Great Law had been codified in the 1400s by Hiawatha and the Peacemaker, with the support of Jigonsaseh, the most powerful of the Clan Matrons. The Iroquois system was (and is) spirit-based. The Council of Matrons was the ceremonial center of the system as well as the prime policymaker. Only sons of eligible clans could serve, at the behest of the Matrons of their clans, on the councils at the executive, legislative, and judicial levels. Public and private life were inseparable and the Matrons had the power to impeach any elected official who was not working for the good of the people.

But when Franklin and others incorporated the Iroquois model into the U.S. Constitution, they omitted women *as a gender*, as well as men of color and men without property. Within fifty years, American Indians were forced onto reservations, declared "alien and dependent" by the U.S. Supreme Court, decimated. The web of their lives was in shreds, seemingly beyond repair. But the Grandmothers of every tribe . . .

I pause here, holding the story in my mind as I listen to vibrations from other strands attached to the abortion controversy. Those strands are economics and politics. At the same time the Supreme Court hurled the rock of its decision through my life, I was reading an article which ostensibly had nothing to with abortion.

The article, from the August issue of *The Atlantic*, is entitled "Kids as Capital." It explores the economic dilemma facing America: an increasingly aged population combined with a decreasing birth rate. Within a generation, the country will be in desperate need of people for the work force and to pay retirement taxes. More babies are needed now. Other industrialized countries have taken a variety of measures to cope with this economic issue. Romania, for example, long had strict laws prohibiting abortion, birth control, and divorce. According to the article, the U.S. government favors "less intrusive" measures, such as tax breaks and/or federal subsidies to parents, which would also help solve the child-poverty problem. Big business, too, is aware of the problem and working toward solutions. In other words, in both sectors, there is growing recognition that "children are the seeds of the people. Seed corn must not be ground." This attitude is good—a hopeful sign of balance and wisdom.

However, although the article stresses the government's concern to develop such policies, implicit in the concept of "kids as capital" is the necessity of women as "breeders" of capital. In the same month that the *Atlantic* article was distributed, the Supreme Court handed down a ruling the effect of which could be to restrict abortion by putting the matter back in the hands of the state. Restrictions on birth control are likely to follow. Breeding stock, by definition, has no choice. It is the property of whoever controls it. Women are being undermined through our bodies. I've heard this story before.

The moral implications of this situation are disturbing enough to contemplate. But I think about Covenant House on the Lower East Side of New York City. This ministry was begun in response to the plight of thousands of street children who—unwanted, homeless, vulnerable—become the capital base of New York's multi-billion-dollar sex industry. Prostitution, pornography, and drugs—for boys and girls. The younger they are, the bigger the profits. Around Times Square, the sex industry is tied in with entertainment, with organized crime, and with large corporations.

Millions of customers—almost exclusively male—patronize the sex industry in New York City and in other cities around the country. Branches of Covenant House are in many of those cities also. The vision of Covenant House is simple: "Kids should not be bought and sold. They should not be exploited. . . . There must

be a place where they can all get help. And when they
need it: before it's too late. And from people who love
and respect them. With no strings. No questions asked.
And in a place where nobody gets excluded."

There are literally tens of thousands of these street
kids in America. Many will be murdered. Many others
will experience a death of the soul that leaves them, for
a while, still breathing. Of the sixteen thousand street
kids who annually make their way to Covenant House
residences around the country, about two thousand
return two or three times "before they make it. Or
before they don't."

While America is in a moral furor over the birth—the
production—of children, the multi-billion-dollar sex
industry grinds on with few challengers. Although
many conscientious people, in my own city and in the
nation, are trying to stop the millstones from grinding—physical and sexual abuse, drugs, poverty,
violence—the force turning the stones seems almost
inexorable.

Who will take care of the seeds of the people? Who
will nurture them to maturity? This is the moral issue
most urgently in need of resolution. At the center of the
interconnected webs—the abortion controversy, the
nation's life, my own life—stand the children who are
among us now. The national web is out of balance,
sagging dangerously. Children feel vibrations from it
every day. They equate love with care. If nurture is
absent, when children are old enough to reason, they
say with clear-eyed honesty, "If you don't want to take
care of us, why did you have us?" Sometimes kids have
God's eyes.

It is possible that we American women will regain

control of our bodies. The Supreme Court decision may eventually be rendered moot—either by the vote of state legislatures or by an influx of the French "morning after pill" (RU485), or by a return to birth control medicines of indigenous peoples, on which American contraceptive research was based. Even so, women will continue to face the issue of our children's welfare and to see the severed ends of the Creator's law still trailing in the wind. It has been two thousand years since Jesus preached the mending of it. Some synagogues and church denominations including my own are trying to bring their structures into harmony with the law. The U.S. Congress is not. Two hundred years have passed since the U.S. Constitution was adopted, fifty-one years since the Equal Rights Amendment was first introduced for debate. Congress remains adamant in refusing to mend the Creator's law, as well as reluctant to make complementary, *enforceable* laws for the siring gender.

I feel virtually powerless. My heart is low. What do I do now? "But the Grandmothers of every tribe . . . " I continue the story—and the hope. In the time of crisis, bereft of political power and disenfranchised in their own land, the Grandmothers felt their hearts sink low. But they did not allow them to be "on the ground." Instead, they took them *underground*, where they joined with wise men, Grandfathers, who accepted women's power as a complement to their own. By restoring the balance of the Creator's law for survival as well as by keeping faith with other sacred laws, American Indians have slowly and patiently rewoven their lives and are emerging with renewed strength.

In most surviving cultures, deep below the turmoil of

historical events, there have been counterparts of the Indian Grandmothers and Grandfathers who, according to their customs, have found ways to ensure that the gender that bears life is not separated from the power to sustain it. Jesus himself upheld this law within a culture whose institutions denied women a policy-making place.

I am continuing to work to restore the Creator's law in all levels of society. Meanwhile, I tell my children the Grandmothers' story. I remind them of the tradition, "Family first—and that includes your people." And I assure them, "Until the seventh generation and beyond—whatever your circumstances—I stand steadfast beside you. I gather you under the wings of my shawl and affirm the wisdom of the Creator, 'Children are the seeds of the people. Seed corn must not be ground.' "

9

Because I Have Been Loved

Jo Kicklighter

Jo Kicklighter has been active for many years in various phases of church work. She has studied feminist theology for almost a decade and counts Christian feminist friends and theologians as some of her major influences during this time. She has spoken on forgotten women in the Christian heritage and on empowering women in local churches. The daughter of a United Methodist minister and the spouse of a retired Navy chaplain, she lives in Pintura, Utah.

Dear Hope,

I know you're a grandchild only "hoped for" now, and I certainly don't know what the world will be like when you read this letter from me; but I do know we have many serious problems in our country, our hemisphere, our planet. Perhaps the most volatile political issue today in the United States is abortion.

Christians differ markedly on abortion. Some claim that abortion is murder, that abortion is always a bad choice, that federal funds should not be used to pay for any abortions. Others say that a woman, not the government, should be able to decide what happens with her body, that a fetus is not a person, that abortion is not always a harmful choice.

I am not convinced there is a right or wrong side for a Christian feminist to be on, but I am trying to be in a "faithful place." I want you to understand how I got to be here and why, for whatever happens in our families, our churches, and our nation about abortion is going to affect you.

My mother and daddy's first child had died at age two, so I was a very much wanted baby. I always felt that I was loved and cherished by parents, grandparents, aunts and uncles. Ours was a Christian family. Daddy was a Methodist minister. Mother was a homemaker and an active churchwoman. I grew up knowing that I was a child of a loving God, as well as a child of my loving parents.

I learned that a baby was a precious gift from God, a source of great joy and delight. But I also found out that if I did "it" before I was married, I might get pregnant and instead of a precious bundle of joy, I would have a sordid bag of shame! Thus, as a teenager, did I first begin to realize one of the great ironies of life—that sex is a major source of human pleasure and a major source of female anxiety!

Today we have more convenient, reliable contraceptives than were available when I came of age. Attitudes about sex have changed. Everywhere we hear and see stories and advertisements which say: Sex is pleasure. Take it and enjoy. Don't think about tomorrow.

It may sound trite, but I believe that my body is "the temple of God"—a gift from the Spirit of Creation, an inextricable part of the totality of my being. I am responsible for how I live in that body, which means that I believe in responsible sexuality. I must use my intelligence in expressing my sexuality, *as much as possible*, by using contraceptives and planning pregnancies.

Your Papa Ed, a Navy chaplain, and I "planned" for our first three children, each two years apart. Then our family life became so hectic that we "planned" *not* to have more children. Nevertheless, before long I was pregnant again, with our "diaphragm baby." *As much as possible.*

It was during those first dark days after learning I was going to have a fourth "bundle of joy and delight" that I personally considered abortion—not for that pregnancy, but should I ever accidentally conceive again. Though abortions were not readily available in the early 1960s, I was certain that I could successfully plead extreme emotional distress. Fortunately I never had to make that decision. I do not think I could have aborted a fetus once I felt life. But if medical tests had indicated the baby would be severely disabled . . . ? Perhaps . . .

You see, Hope, I can't think of abortion in terms of abstract principles only, but in terms of *persons* in real-life situations. And I remember that Jesus was concerned about *persons* in real-life situations.

What if my daughter, Laurie, had become pregnant as a teenager? I would have wanted her to be able to *choose* between safe abortion, adoption, or raising the child herself. What if Laurie, now married, should become pregnant while taking a powerful prescription drug which would cause the fetus to be damaged? Once again, I am grateful she can choose safe abortion.

I can still see the tortured eyes in the pale face and hear the wrenching sobs of a young friend I met at a workshop. A victim of incest, she was struggling valiantly to find her way through a storm of conflicting emotions to health and wholeness. What if she had become pregnant with her own father's child? Yes, I would have wanted *her* to be able to choose abortion.

I think of Marie,* almost like a daughter, who fled the terror of life with her promiscuous, mentally ill mother to the Navy and soon the relative comfort of marriage to a domineering, self-centered man. How she fought for identity and confirmation of her own intelligence and sanity! While in medical school, she became pregnant. She did not want to bring a child into the destructive marital environment; she needed to continue her education; she felt she *had* to choose abortion. "It was like sacrificing one for the sake of many," she said. As

---

*Not her real name.

an innovative, sensitive physicians's assistant, she has been able to help many people. I am thankful she could choose safe abortion.

Fresh in my memory is another personal story told from the floor of a business session of our denomination's General Assembly this year. A resolution written in opposition to a recent anti-abortion ruling by the Supreme Court was being discussed. A youthful ordained minister came to a microphone and poured out her story, heretofore shared only with her counselor. She had been raped. An abortive drug routinely administered in post-rape care had "gone wrong." The fetus lived, but was doomed to be cruelly deformed. Her voice almost breaking with emotion, she spoke of her agonizing decision to abort the fetus. For she did *not* "believe in" abortion. But what right did she have to bring into the world a child doomed to a miserable life of institutional care? Abortion was her prayerful Christian choice. She was thankful she could *make* that choice.

If *I* were in the childbearing years, I would not want any government to tell me whether or not I could continue a pregnancy just as I don't think a man would want any government to tell him whether or not he could have a vasectomy. And so I want other women to be able also to *choose* to have a legal, safe abortion. I also think that laws which make it impossible for poor women to get abortions seem un-Christian, for women with money will always be able to get safe abortions somewhere. And I resent the fact that people who do not "believe in" abortion have pre-empted the title "pro-life," for I also am *for life*. I am for a *"wanted"* life for all children.

But given all of that, the question still is: What am *I* doing, from my faithful place, regarding abortion?

I try to stay informed. I am a member of, and give money to, organizations which support what I perceive to be the responsible Christian position. I talk to friends and family about abortion issues and questions. I mail cards to legislators. I discuss related resolutions with delegates to denominational meetings.

When working with women's groups in the church, I encourage women to tell their stories, to see themselves as created "in the image of God," and to continue their personal and spiritual growth.

As a Sunday school teacher and music leader, I try to choose materials which express thankfulness for life and stimulate children to act responsively and responsibly as "stewards" of creation.

I pray for all women who have undesired pregnancies and face difficult decisions regarding those pregnancies.

I pray for myself, that I may respect those whose views about abortion are different from mine.

Finally, I pledge that I shall continue to support organizations, legislators, church groups, educators, writers, businesses, parents, grandparents, counselors—all those who strive for full personhood and equal rights for women and men and children and youth, able and differently-able, of all races and ethnic backgrounds.

For, after all, didn't Jesus talk about "abundant life" as if *everybody* would want it?

Thanks for reading this long letter. I hope you understand.

Love,
Mama Jo

10

David and Bathsheba Have a Word for Us

Roberta Kells Dorr

Roberta Kells Dorr writes historical novels set primarily in biblical times. She has long been interested in foreign missions and has lived in Gaza and in Yemen, where she has done research for her writing. Her work has been published by Chosen Books, Bantam, Harper & Row, and Broadman. *David and Bathsheba* was selected for the Guideposts Book Club. She holds a B.A. in creative writing from the University of Maryland and a master's degree in religious education from Southern Baptist Seminary. She gained many insights into the lives of historical and biblical characters when she lived in a little village where women washed their clothes in the stream, went to the well for water, and lived in harems of three or more wives.

As a writer of historical novels, I find it much easier to get a proper perspective on people and situations of the distant past than on those of our own day. I can quickly see just how those people should have faced personal or even national problems. If they happened to be Christians, it is even easier to draw up the lines of approval and disapproval.

For instance, in Bible times and in many countries today, it has been traditional for the whole community to punish adultery by stoning the woman. This was a reaction not just by religious people, but by members of the whole community. Adultery was a threat to the stability of the community, and so the community took violent action.

In this setting, we see Jesus taking a strangely new approach. He didn't say adultery was all right; in fact he labeled it sin. But then he moved on very quickly to minister to the victim. What strange words we hear him say, "Neither do I condemn thee, go and sin no more."

His approach was new and startling. The people who watched felt there must be something wrong with it. It didn't sound right. They felt that he, being a religious person, a teacher and rabbi, should have joined in the stoning.

Now I have done a great deal of thinking about this. Is there some clue here, some common ground, on which we Christians can unite? We will always have Christians who are violently against abortion and equally dedicated Christians who see it a bit differently.

Is it possible that in spite of our differences we can join together in ministering to the victims?

Who are the victims? you may be asking. For a long time you may have been thinking only of the unborn child as victim, but is there not more which God's Holy Spirit would have us see? I first got a glimpse of these "other" victims at a convention where I was speaking to members of the Christian Booksellers Association.

I had been asked to speak on the writing of my novel *David and Bathsheba*. The novel is an attempt to put together the pieces of David's life as he related to the woman he loved and yet the woman who involved him in both adultery and murder. In writing this historical novel I had explored every aspect of guilt and its devastating consequences. I had come to realize that guilt is probably the most debilitating, degrading, and destructive emotion that mankind is capable of experiencing. I had also come to realize that its destructive force was the very thing that God had been actively battling on our behalf since the beginning of time.

This was the problem Jesus tackled head on with his death on the cross. However, the period I wrote about was back in 1000 B.C., in the time of David and the Kingdom of Israel. Who would think that the people of that far distant day could bring hope and new life to a twentieth-century captive of the same debilitating force of guilt?

I'll never forget that night. I had finished speaking and was standing out in the hall talking to various people who had gathered around to ask questions. I noticed that on the edge of the crowd was a beautiful young woman who seemed anxious to see me.

I was tired and there were friends waiting for me;

however, I couldn't resist the look in her eyes. She obviously had something to tell me.

She waited patiently until the others had gone and then she grabbed my arm. "I know you're busy, but I must tell you what reading your novel did for me."

I smiled, expecting some nice words of encouragement. "I'm glad the novel has meant so much to you," I said.

"You don't understand," she insisted. "This novel changed my life. I have to tell you what happened."

We found seats at one side of the auditorium, and she began the story. "Before I was a Christian, I had an affair that ended in a pregnancy. I didn't want to marry the man, and to have a child at that time seemed impossible; so I had an abortion. I felt I had no other choice, and I dismissed it from my mind and thought no more about it.

"Some years later I became a Christian, not just a nominal Christian but a genuinely born-again Christian. Soon after this happened, I met a wonderful young man and we were married. He was all that I had ever wanted in a husband. He was a dedicated Christian, a talented, loving person, and I was very much in love. I told him about the abortion and then we both dismissed it as something out of my past. A pre-Christian past that was now over and gone.

"I became active in church and selling Christian books. For the first time in my life I was happy and fulfilled. Then it happened. Suddenly and without warning. We were just leaving our hotel to attend the evening meeting of our annual Booksellers' convention. One minute I was excited and animatedly discussing the meeting, and the next plunged into a depression that was to last for months.

"The reason for this drastic change came as quite a surprise. I had noticed outside the convention hall some anti-abortion women marching and carrying posters. It was one of the posters that jolted me into the severe depression. The poster was of a fetus quite vividly pictured. I glanced at it quickly and was about to turn away when my attention was drawn to the small, very human hands. I stood rooted to the ground while my heart raced wildly and a veritable flood of emotions pummeled me.

"Those hands were real hands. That was a real little person, not just some plastic toy or fatty tissue. I must have let out a moan because my husband turned back and came to see what was the matter. I couldn't speak. I couldn't tell him what was wrong. It was something I wasn't even able to put into words.

"He saw that I was too traumatized to go to the meeting and so he took me back to our room. Here I paced the floor and wept. I tried to tell him what had happened. He was bewildered. We had discussed the abortion. That was in the past. Why, then, was I so devastated by some little hands on a poster?

" 'You've seen posters like that before,' he said. 'I don't understand why you are so upset. It's something that's over, in the past; you've been forgiven for whatever you've done.'

"Everything he said was true. I knew with my mind that he was right, but that didn't heal the deep, gut feeling of loss, irretrievable loss, I was experiencing. I couldn't explain. I didn't even know how to get at the hurt. It was just there, a steady, constant ache that was destroying my happiness.

"I didn't go to any of the meetings. I stayed in that hotel room and tried to deal with this monster from the past. I rationalized, theorized, and finally just made up my mind I wouldn't let it bother me. Nothing worked, and before I fully realized it, I was in the throes of a major depression.

"Of course I tried counseling and even exercise. We went on a vacation, but nothing helped. I knew that if it continued I would not only lose my mind but my husband also.

"Then I got your book, *David and Bathsheba*. It was one of the new books we would be selling that spring. I always read the new books so I could answer questions and comment intelligently.

"I found it to be a good story, and before many pages I was caught up in the action. Then a strange, miraculous thing happened. I had completely identified with David and Bathsheba. As David took Bathsheba, even though she was another man's wife, and then instigated the murder of her husband, I empathized completely. I felt that I was there with them when their child died—and the terrible guilt that descended on them. Then, just as I had identified with David in his guilt, I found myself identifying with his restoration. I'll never forget it.

"Here," she said, taking the book from me. "It's on pages 282 and 283. It's where David went up to Mt. Moriah and built an altar. The words of his prayer described exactly how I felt. His thoughts were very much like mine.

" 'Surely I have sinned,' " she read, " 'more than

117

these my brethren. How can the blood of these oxen take away the guilt and shame that I carry in my heart?'

"Then," she said, "I read God's words to him and I noticed that it said, 'God spoke to him gently. "You are guilty," he said, "and I have decreed that every sin must be punished. But because I have loved you with an everlasting love, I have provided a substitute, if you will take it. See now, these oxen. I have decreed that every sin placed on these oxen will no longer rest on you. You will go free. The Lord your God does not mean for you to be forever burdened with this guilt." '

"You pictured David doing just that and as he did what God told him to do, he was freed of his guilt. I suddenly realized that I too had that option. It would have never occurred to me that I could put my sins on Jesus. It just didn't seem right. But that was what God was saying. He had provided release. I had only to accept it.

"I knelt by the bed and did just what David had done, and the same release came to me. I could hardly believe it. I was free. I knew I no longer had to carry that guilt. I didn't understand how it was done anymore than David understood, but I knew that by accepting it, I was free.

"It has been almost a year now and the guilt and depression have never returned. My marriage has been restored, and my life is full and meaningful."

There were tears in her eyes, but they were happy tears. She squeezed my hand, "I just wanted you to know, what happened to David so long ago happened to me."

I never did get her name, but I won't forget her. I

learned something very important that day. I learned that there are hurting people out there who desperately need the good news that Jesus came to give. We dare not as Christians get so busy determining the right and wrong of things that we forget our glorious message.

As Christian women we can all be united in this one mission, this mission which was Jesus' "to bind up the brokenhearted, to proclaim freedom for the captives and release from darkness for the prisoners, . . . to comfort all who mourn, . . . to bestow on them a crown of beauty instead of ashes, the oil of gladness instead of mourning, and a garment of praise instead of a spirit of despair" (Isaiah 61:1-3 NIV).

Back in my room that night, I thought again of the young woman's story. I realized that most of us were caught up in the abstract rightness or wrongness of abortion and were often forgetful of compassion. Jesus himself never fought for legislation that would change the world, but rather was busy binding up the wounds, healing hurts and spreading the "good news," that the debt was paid. There was no more condemnation.

11

In Him Was Life, John 1:4

Sandra O. Smithson, O.S.F.

Sister Sandra Smithson is a graduate of Xavier University in New Orleans. Prior to entering the School Sisters of St. Francis in 1953, she hosted a daily radio show, "A Woman Speaks." She has done course work at Creighton University; Alverno College, Milwaukee; University of Wisconsin; Catholic University of Puerto Rico; and the University of Costa Rica. She has been an English teacher, a hospital superior, and a college principal.

The nation had not completely settled down from the shake-up that followed the Civil Rights battles of the sixties which led to the extension of legal protection for Blacks, in the Civil Rights Act of 1968, before it was threatened with once more being split asunder just five years later, in 1973, in the *Roe v. Wade* decision which took legal protection away from the unborn in the first trimester of gestation. For the first time in the nation's history, private citizens, outside the consideration of self-defense, would be given the legal right to destroy the life of another. It was a wrenching decision that propelled the nation into a struggle akin to civil war. Today as I write, the battle lines are drawn in public debates, marches, demonstrations, threats, and even bombings. So polarized is the nation, so large the issue, so heated the emotions it engenders, that families are split asunder and political fortunes, no matter the other merits of a candidate, can be made or destroyed on this single issue alone.

At the core of the conflict is a clash of rights: the woman's right to privacy, her control over her own body, versus the right of the fetus to life and protection until it can exist independently of the woman's womb.

The conflict is packaged euphemistically as pro-choice or pro-life. The pro-life people are those who are seen as willing to trample on the rights of women, as willing to reduce the woman to nothing more than a vessel for the gestation of the male seed, as indifferent to the health and life of women. The pro-choice people are viewed as those who are willing to commit or condone murder, those who will allow women to place whatever selfish personal choices above that of the right of something so important as human life to survive. To pro-lifers, pro-choicers are destroyers of human life at its most vulnerable: the child in the womb. To pro-choicers, pro-lifers are destroyers of human rights at their most fundamental: a woman's right to control how her own body will be used.

The rending of the nation that occurred during the Civil Rights Movement resulted in the treatment of a sore that had festered too long in the body politic and the excising of which promised to lead to greater national health. The abortion issue, however, no matter what the law, threatens only to deepen the nation's wounds and lead to greater national illness.

Of course, *Roe v. Wade* did not create the abortion issue. Abortion had a way of touching many lives long before the issue was a matter of generalized public debate. In my own life, abortion touched me for the first time when, as a pre-schooler, I overheard the gossip of nosy neighbors critical of my mother: "I thought she'd die with Sandra. Wouldn't you think she'd quit now? One day, one of those pregnancies will take her away from here. And she won't let me help her get rid of any of them." My mother's response to suggestions that she start aborting was simple and direct. "God alone has the power to create life; God alone should have the right to destroy it." It was my first poignant lesson in "respect for life." Nevertheless, with the four subsequent births that followed my own, I lived in quiet fear of my mother's possible impending death.

Abortion touched my life when I was in elementary school and the teenage daughter of a neighbor lay dying from the botched attempt of a butcher to help her abort an unwanted fetus, conceived out of wedlock. The story was that she died from pleurisy brought on by eating green apples. But we kids, somehow, all knew. Later, the grown folks recounted how her life ebbed away while she continued to cry out, "I don't want to die! I don't want to die!"

In high school, it touched my life again. A dear and trusted friend was dismissed from her parental home because, at sixteen, she had become pregnant and refused to have an abortion. Abandoned by her family and the forty-five-year-old man who had impregnated her in the process of satisfying his own lust, she and the son she bore roamed the streets of the city, swelling the homeless statistics and bearing the burden of society's rejection of her as a "fallen" woman. We continued our friendship in alley entrances and old, abandoned houses until the day I went away to college. When I came home for my first Christmas vacation, she wasn't there anymore. I never saw her again.

During my years as a teaching Franciscan nun, abortion would touch my life more than once in the lives of my students. Their anguish would become my anguish; their pain, my pain. With some, I walked the seven-month pilgrimage from the second month following the night of illicit pleasure to the pleasure of completed birth, only to grieve with them through the pain of separation as they handed over into the adopting arms of another the life they had made and so lovingly nurtured. With yet others, it was a time of angry wrangling as they attempted to wrestle from me, if not consent, then, at least, a sympathetic under-standing of why it was better in their cases to abort than to give birth. With these, the accusation always surfaced: "How can you understand? After all, how can a celibate nun know anything about sex and pregnancy, or what to do when they shouldn't have happened? Only the person involved can know."

On many such occasions, because of my celibate life-style, my empathy was held suspect. Yet celibacy, far from alienating me, had more greatly sensitized me to the problem, for the life of celibacy had moved me beyond preoccupation with the particularities of my own private concerns and had drawn me ever deeper into the pains and burdens of the total human experience. Indeed, it was this growing awareness of our human solidarity that enabled me to choose the life of celibacy in the first place.

Still, on more than one occasion, my attempts to enter the abortion debate have been rejected on the grounds that my life-style made me unqualified. It is testimony to the profundity of our estrangement from one another that we have come to view the individuation implied by personhood and the social categories achieved through vocation/career differentiation as sufficient to rupture the commonality and unity of the human experience. Too little of the abortion debate is cast in this larger context. Rather, much is tied to "legality" and "personal privacy and individual rights." Much is tied to the question of "planned parenthood" for reasons of economics, personal convenience, career choices, or the merits of abortion as a method of birth control. Much is made of the manner in which the pregnancy occurred: rape, incest. Much is made of the age of the impregnated woman or the threat the pregnancy portends to her health and/or life.

And something, too, is made of the condition of the fetus. But very little, if any, of the debate is based on the reality of our *common human vocation*. So far have we destroyed in our consciousness the awareness of our unity, of our oneness, of our interrelatedness and interdependence in this experience of shared human life that we can decide that the destruction of human life, whether in potentiality or already actualized, can be regarded as a personal and private matter of choice.

Yet, in many matters of lesser weight, the "common good" receives consideration over private rights. For example, even the most conscientious guardians of free speech would not condone shouting in the critical care unit of a hospital, or a fun-filled bellow of "Fire!" in a crowded theater. And I know of no time when private property rights remained sacrosanct in the face of a state or city project designed to benefit the larger community. How many times have we witnessed, in one way or another, the forced removal of an old man or woman from his or her home of many years because a piece of property is in the path of a proposed freeway? If, then, there is precedent in conventional law for considering the common good over private rights even at purely natural and pragmatic levels related to human living, how much more so should such a principle apply in matters of human life itself.

All issues that impact upon the question of *life* are interconnected and must be viewed in a larger context than the mere legal question of individual rights. Issues affecting *human life*, at whatever level, are issues of moral and ethical magnitude and necessarily transcend conventional law. And when viewed from this perspective, the general common good is a far weightier imperative than the perceived rights of the individual. What stands in the way of our sympathy for this point of view is the ever-growing secularization of our social decisions. Under the pretext of favoring no religion as demanded by the Constitution, we have moved from being "one nation under God" to being a disconnected plurality of rugged individuals in pursuit of private, material gain at the expense of the good of the whole.

Beyond every other consideration is the will of the One who is Architect of the universe and the plan for all that comes from that divine, creative Source. To a secular world, the view from the position of supernatural faith is meaningless. Nevertheless, while human life, natural though it is, transcends natural power to create it, faith becomes a reasonable approach in dealing with the issues that impact upon such life.

In the divine dispensation, it would seem that God's highest creative action was to bring into existence beings in the divine image through whom the glory of that divinity could be extended into visible creation. For as the divine nature is the source of unity in the trinitarian Godhead, so human nature, comprising as it does all the elements of which the visible and invisible creation is composed, becomes the source of unity of all creation. Therefore, the Incarnation Event, whereby the divine nature is joined to human nature, allows for the possibility of all creation to be subsumed once more to the Source from whence it came. This position of human nature, special and lofty as it is, nevertheless is not without serious consequences, for it negates in the individual human being the possibility of purely private action. Whatever the seeming privacy of human behavior, it is socialized to impact on humanity as a whole. This is the reality that made possible our inheritance of death through the disobedience of our first parents and our restoration to *life* through the obedience of the Savior. Between these two special primal vocations, and demonstrated by them, is the principle of solidarity that governs all human behavior. Therefore, couching the abortion debate in questions relating to "privacy" or "individual rights" is to guarantee the "abortion" of any solution related to it.

The final question to be explored, then, is what makes human life so important to God? In writing of God, St. John says, "In Him was *Life* ," and in writing of the creation of the human species, the author of Genesis says, "He breathed into them the *Breath of Life*." This Breath of Life implied something more than simply raising to an organic state the dust out of which humanity was created. The organic state already existed in creation. Simple evolution was sufficient for its perpetuation. This Breath of Life then, was something more. It was something akin to that Life in God alone, referred to by St. John, for Genesis continues: "and man [the human person] became a *living soul*." And it is precisely this that makes human life so important to God, for it exists to be a receptacle for the extension of divine life beyond the Godhead itself. That is why the Mother of Jesus, greeted by the Angel as "full of grace" (that is, filled with the Breath of God's Life), could respond in all humility, "My soul magnifies the Lord!"

In this transcendent scenario, the creation and nurturing of human life becomes the highest of all human vocations because it makes possible the "magnification" of the Life of God beyond himself. The logical conclusion, then, is that the abortion of human life becomes one of the most detestable of all human acts.

But the problem of abortion should not be limited to a discussion of the unborn fetus, which is partially a question related to the quantification of human life, but must be extended to embrace the quality of all human life from conception to death. Every human being who deliberately acts to frustrate the realization of another person's full human potential is an abortionist. Hence, all aggression, abuse, racism, sexism, and whatever other truncating behavior, places the perpetrator in direct opposition to the divine will, for in a truncated personality, the "Divine Life" cannot be fully magnified.

Therefore, a nation in which the destruction of human life, at whatever stage of development, is accepted, a nation in which things are valued over persons, a nation that caters to the whims of individuals without regard for the common good, a nation that disavows responsibility for the quality of life of its citizens, a nation that does not protect the weak and the vulnerable, such a nation, for its part and its purposes, may attest as does ours, "In God we trust"; but God, for His part and His purposes, cannot trust in such a nation.

Though We Walk Through the Valley of the Shadow of Death:
A Conclusion

Phyllis Tickle

Phyllis Tickle is the author of *Final Sanity, Ordinary Time,* and *What the Heart Already Knows,* published by The Upper Room, and *The Tickle Papers,* published by Abingdon Press. She contributed to the *365 Meditations for Women* (Abingdon). A lector and vestrywoman in the Episcopal Church, she has served on her diocesan task force on abortion.

This book began with my saying that each of the twelve of us had her own story to tell. Then as editor, I opened the collection with a story of my own, one intended to offer a context for the others which follow. You now have read those eleven others, and I would ask that you read one more. I want to add one final story; for you see, I stand as a contributor at the end of our collection by virtue of my age, and not by virtue of my job description.

It was October 1967 and the boy sitting across from me was scarcely ten years my junior, but his words would make us both old before he was done with me.

His name was John, and he was the first of my boys to come in with the words. Before it was over, there would be seven more sitting where John sat now, seven more speaking the words that were to make a pieta of my womanhood.

I had been in that office for almost four years as academic dean, an unusual job in the American 1960s for a woman, but then ours was an unusual school, a college of art where every rule except the truth was suspect and every cultural bias subject to piercing dissection. "My" first class, the first group of students whom I had known from entrance to exit, would graduate B.F.A. in late May, the first group of the gifted whom I had admitted to freshman composition and had hovered over through Western Civilization and counseled toward the successful completion of our ominous requirements in foreign language. By graduation day in the spring, most of them would have been in at least one of my own classes, and all of them would have been in my office with a problem, a frustration, sometimes with just a joy, but most often with a mother-hunger.

That, of course, was the cultural bias the college had looked at before it had offered me the position as its academic officer. It had concluded that all human beings need to touch the feminine as well as the masculine in their day-to-day commerce and that all human beings need the solace which it is the unique property of women to create and share.

That morning, the solace was frozen within me by the horror. It could not reach across that suddenly vast desk to John; it could not even reach across the interior to warm me.

"I'm going over the border to Canada now," he was saying. "They are waiting for me outside in the car. I'll be across by midnight tomorrow."

The eyes, big, black as the Italian hair and long lashes that described his features, looked up at me for the first time, and I saw the panic. A boy making a man's decision and asking a woman's blessing, the traveling icon of a mother's benediction. I could not give it. I could not even discover the borders where benediction lay.

The brown hands, Mediterranean as the rest of him and scuffed hard from years at the potter's wheel, wound and rewound themselves in the valley of his open knees. Outside in the hall the natural sounds of a college approaching mid-term rose and fell with the flow of student traffic and administrative bustle. Only in our private hell was all existence arrested.

"I don't want you to do anything," he said at last. And I understood that the few moments of spontaneity when I could have done anything were ended. He leaned back in the chair, sat up straighter and crossed his legs, no longer the supplicant, no longer hopeful for anything from outside himself. He pulled the letter out of his pocket, the thin government issue paper belying the austerity of the seal of the President of the United States of America.

"I can't kill," he said.

I nodded and could feel myself nodding, could feel the separation from myself which let me see myself nodding as well as him accepting.

"I didn't want you to know in time to be able to do anything. I can't tell President Burrows and Mr. Lowe, because they would think they had to try to stop me, but I'd like them to know tomorrow how much this place has meant to me, how much I appreciate it all. Would you tell them for me?"

I nodded dumbly.

"Also my folks?" He hesitated and the hands began to move again. Finally, they sought and found, not each other, but the arms of the chair he was sitting in. "My dad was Korea, and he won't ever understand this—can't even see why it's different. And my mom is tied to whatever he says. She has to be to stay with him. You understand, don't you?"

I did.

"I'll write you," he said, "just as soon as I get there—to let you know I made it okay and didn't get caught. Okay?"

The paralysis was ending somewhere deep below, somewhere where my thoughts did not usually go. Pain was burning away amazement like a rush of brandy through the nearly frozen. I reached across the desk and its clutter of papers to lay my hand upon one of his. Quickly, gratefully, like a lover rather than a boy, his other hand was laid over both of ours. "Oh, God," his voice caught for the first time. Then he broke the clasp, stood up and was to the door before I could rise. Just as he closed it behind him, he looked at me one more time. "I just wish they had let me graduate first." And he was gone.

I sat in the office with the door closed for two hours, ignoring the knocks, the phone rings, the intercom, and the notes slipped under the door. I sat buying John time by my own inertia. Unable to sanction what he was doing and unable to initiate anything that would prevent it, I sat. Nero fiddled, Madame Defarge knitted, I stared at the wall.

And it never got any better. Oh, the staring ended finally. I went to my lecture room and, like a professional, I taught a decent enough class. The next morning I went into the president's office with one message and over to pottery's central office with another. I answered coolly one phone call from an irate first-generation American whose pride had been crushed beyond fatherhood into wrath. Later, almost at quitting time, I wept with the first-generation American mother, whose gasps could not distort the music of the Italian accents which punctuated her litany. On Monday of the next week the letter came, airmail and covered in the pastel stamps of the Canadian postal system. John had made it.

Because John stayed in Canada, I never saw him again. But I have never stopped seeing him; nor have I ever been able to purge from insistent memory the image of that autumnal office with his words and my nodding head. In time and in dulled mourning, I have come to accept the fact that nodding and staring were all that John had expected of me and that the ancient blessing of "Go in peace," which in my confusion I had denied him, was the most that he had hoped for as well as the limit of what he had needed. The moral issues of Vietnam had moved into the vast and unindividuated stadium of American political life long before John had had to make his private decision, and neither he nor I nor anyone else could have stayed the grinding process of that carnage.

It is unique to modern experience that every side of a moral dilemma, once we have allowed an issue to slip into the public arena, must be politicized by the rhetoric of what we discover is expected of us by the majority of our peers rather than by what we can agree is required of us by our God. But in a small office in a small college, a boy named John, abandoned by a culture in chaos and bereft of even my woman's benediction, had to cast his private vote on the solitary basis of who he understood himself to be and what he believed he could accept himself as becoming.

In the decade which followed, John's vote would be joined by thousands of others until, action by action, decision by decision, their columns were tallied and the moral stances of American culture rendered too individual to be redemptive of the adult community that had parented the ranks of the voting. Vietnam's was to become the first blood spilled without integrity in our history, and the taste of it, the ferrous odor of its decay in the sands of our politics, has informed every issue of our people in the two and a half decades since.

Now in another time, with another generation and

through the anguish of another sex, we move inexorably and once again toward non-resolution about the deliberate ending of life. Once again we shed blood without purchase, leaving the issues of our identity unresolved and the labor of any change unengaged.

Like several of my fellow essayists here, I believe abortion as a political issue is moribund. The abortifacient RU485 will complete, within our time, the privatizing of the issue in much the same way that the Canadian border completed the isolation of decision and consequence for John and his generation. But neither borders nor privacy is the issue which concerns me.

Vietnam was John to me, for I could, and did, touch and embrace and lose him. Abortion also is embrace and loss, but unlike Vietnam, it must not be allowed to dwindle away without honesty. This time, we must make purchase from the blood and the silent screams of both our babies and our daughters.

In that tragic minute when John said to me, "My dad was Korea and he won't ever understand this," he told me everything; and of all his words, those are the ones which have stayed most firmly locked into my memory during the years since he said them to me. The warrior father and the domestic mother could not self-immolate. They could not reject the roles by which they had defined themselves. They could not condemn to change the all-beneficent, all-powerful empire that had entranced their own parents. They could not refute the necessity of the expansion which fed and entertained them, nor could they risk the loss of that grandeur with which they assuaged the void of their Babbittry. They could not, and so they offered their son instead.

We offered all our sons. We offered them as scapegoats and their blood as expiation. Not with knife and priest as in the old days, of course, but with our rhetoric we threw them to the conflicting values we could not resolve and to the paradoxes we dared not address. "You decide," we said to them and then made their decision impossible by declaring every decision wrong, unacceptable, morally repugnant.

And in our shedding of their blood, in the heat of our anger and in the depths of our sorrow, we bought that precious distance which lay between ourselves and either guilt or mercy. "See, my son, how badly you—defector and soldier alike—have chosen, and see how your error has wounded me." It is that perfidious distance and its seductive horror which haunt me.

"Christian, what now of your Christianity?"

We twelve may not have answered well, but each of us has answered prayerfully and candidly.

Each of us asks that the question itself be dearer to you than our words.

As for me, I would dedicate my own words not to my children, but to John and his generation in the hope that their agony and that of our daughters may now find some translation into wisdom, may at last give us some purchase with which to forgive and accept ourselves.

Let us go in peace.